So You've Got
A GREAT
IDEA

So You've Got
A GREAT
IDEA

Steve Fiffer

PERSEUS BOOKS

Reading, Massachusetts

Library of Congress Cataloging-in-Publication Data

Fiffer, Steve.
  So you've got a great idea.

  Includes index.
  1. New business enterprises.   I. Title.
H62.5.F53   1986   658.1'1   85-26701
ISBN 0–201–11536–0

Text design by Anna Post
Set in 11 point Sabon by Compset, Inc., Beverly, Mass.

Perseus Books is a member of the
Perseus Books Group

18 19 20 21 22—020100

To Sharon
Marrying you was my greatest idea.

ACKNOWLEDGEMENTS

I would like to thank the following people for their invaluable assistance: John Arado, Jane Jordan Browne, Robin Manna, Robert Rifkin, Gladys Riskind, Jeff Robinson, Genoa Shepley, Joseph Shipley, Nancy Smith, John Svoboda, Bill Warner, Sharon Fiffer, and all of the entrepreneurs profiled on these pages.

Contents

CONTENTS

Part 1

ORDINARY PEOPLE, EXTRAORDINARY IDEAS

1

So You've Got
a Great
Idea

The vitality of thought is in adventure. Ideas won't keep. Something must be done about them.
— ALFRED NORTH WHITEHEAD

All progress is based on a universal innate desire on the part of every organism to live beyond its income.
— SAMUEL BUTLER

Not too long ago, my wife came home from her exercise class feeling extremely frustrated. "It's embarrassing being bigger than everyone else there," she lamented.

"You just had a baby," I reminded her. "You *should* look bigger than everyone else."

"I know that, and you know that," she said. "But the people in the class, at the club, on the street, they don't know that. If my sweatshirt just said 'Postpartum' or something . . . ."

The seed of an idea had just been planted.

A few days later my wife shared her unhappiness with another woman who also had recently given birth. "Exercise-wear is hardly the problem," said the woman. "Where can you find flattering clothing that's also comfortable and practical?"

3

The seed was growing.

The next morning my wife was very excited. "I've got an idea!" she exclaimed. "Let's market a line of clothing for women like me who've just had babies and can't wear what they used to wear."

The seed had germinated.

I am a lawyer. The practical, analytical me came forth. "How do you know there isn't already such a line?" I asked, then continued without waiting for an answer, "And when are you going to do this? You're going back to work in a month. There's the baby. . . ."

I don't think she heard me. "We'll have a sweatshirt that says 'Postpartum,' a skirt with an elastic waist, a smock-type shirt with pockets for bottles and nipples and such and little snaps that you can hook things onto. Everything will have style, feel good, look good, and be washable. The baby can spit up as many times as she likes without spoiling it!"

Ah, the vitality of thought! Ah, the prospect of living beyond our current income!

Subsequent conversations with several other mothers of young children and a superficial perusal of clothing stores and mail-order catalogs convinced me my wife might be onto something. There seemed to be a need for such a line, and there didn't appear to be anyone addressing the specific audience with the need. But while I was becoming a convert, my wife was having second thoughts. Not about the idea. She remained convinced of its validity. Following through was what gave her pause. "Coming up with the idea seems to have been the easiest part," she confessed. "What do I do next? What do you do once you have a great idea?"

"Go to the library or the bookstore and find a book that tells you what to do," I advised, kindly resisting the urge to bill her for this sage legal advice.

We went together. We found books on how to protect an idea and patent an invention; but these books didn't tell us what to do next. We found books on how to start your own business; but my wife wasn't sure she wanted to start her own business. Maybe it would make more sense to go to an existing business and work out an arrangement. Maybe she could just sell the idea to someone better equipped and with more time and resources.

In short, extensive research revealed that while several books provided various pieces to the puzzle confronting my wife, there was no bible to which she could turn — no one book that laid out everything. In addition, those piecemeal texts that did exist were rather dry and tedious. They seemed to reduce the exciting process of bringing an idea to fruition to a lecture on the ins and outs of accounting.

And thus was born another idea. The idea for this book.

Fueled both by the adventure of thought and the desire for profit, the spirit of innovation is alive and well in America today. My wife is hardly alone in her creativity or confusion. Almost every person I talk to has at one time or another come up with what he or she thinks is the next million-dollar idea. These persons who have been struck by the muse of innovation are not Harvard M.B.A.'s or professional inventors, but everyday people like you and me. They are men and women of all ages, and they come from all walks of life — the home, academia, blue-collar and white-collar America.

But if the *spirit* of creativity is alive and well, I'm not sure the actual *practice* is. Unfortunately, for many people, coming up with an idea represents the end rather than the beginning of a process. Either we share the idea with spouse or friends, receive their accolades, and bask for a time in the glory of being deemed "clever" or "creative," or we bemoan the fact that we lack the skill or time to do something that could be both fulfilling and profitable. The moaning becomes even more intense when we later read that someone else has successfully turned "our" idea into a reality, or we realize that the time for our idea has come and gone. "Ideas are like milk. They have a limited shelf life," says Owen Ryan, the founder of General Comet Industries, a company that has the audacity to bill itself as "The Official Representative of Halley's Comet."

This book is intended to inspire and inform you so that your great ideas do not go sour. It addresses the doubts we all have when deciding whether or not to turn an idea into a reality, and it examines the wide range of possibilities open to us — starting a full-time business, setting up a part-time concern, working out of the home, taking the idea to an existing business and working out an arrangement, or selling the idea outright.

I have divided the presentation into two parts, which are followed by a Resource Guide. Part One tells the stories of several individuals who have turned specific ideas into successful enterprises. One of these individuals told me, "The experience was so exciting. You should make this into a screenplay."

Indeed, many of the stories told here contain all of the necessary elements for dramatic presentation. But I offer them for more than entertainment. On the following pages you will meet a diverse group of characters. Among them are Ann and Mike Moore. While serving in the Peace Corps in Togo, West Africa, this Colorado couple observed that infants gently strapped to their mothers' bodies were extremely content. Returning to the States in the early 1960s, the Moores looked for something that would allow them to carry their new daughter in similar fashion. Unable to find anything, they designed and eventually marketed the universally acclaimed Snugli. You will also meet Lynn Tatar, a housewife and mother whose chocolate creations so impressed family and friends that they persuaded her to create a profitable candy company; and Duvall Hecht, a former Olympic gold medalist who grew so tired of listening to pop music on the radio as he commuted to work that he founded the highly successful and much-imitated Books on Tape.

These individuals and the many others profiled all started at square one with an idea. Many had no business experience; most had little capital. V. R. "Swede" Roskam is another one of the innovators you will meet. Roskam took the basic principles of bartering and developed an organization that generates over a million dollars a year in scholarships for needy students. Before coming up with the idea, he had no experience in the barter field. But he claims this deficiency was never cause for alarm. "I saw that the people who did have experience put their pants on one leg at a time, just like I did," he says.

The steps taken by Roskam and the others I profile, the lessons they learned, the advice they give — all are instructive to those of us who are trying to decide what to do with our own great ideas — start a new venture, sell the idea, or join forces with an existing business. These profiles will focus on different kinds of ideas — ideas for products, services, novelties, and business establishments; ideas for ventures that can be performed out of the home; ideas requiring part-time effort; and ideas for not-for-profit organizations.

Whereas these profiles will provide you with a basic understanding of what is involved in following through on particular kinds of ideas and what course you should pursue, Part Two explains how to follow through and how it feels to follow through. Turning an idea into a reality is a risky proposition. Each year, more new businesses fail than flourish. I offer this information not to deter you from pursuing your idea, but to suggest that the euphoria of the creative process must be tempered by the sobriety of good business practice. Some ideas fail simply because the innovator did not exercise sound business judgment. Chapter 9 therefore presents the nuts and bolts of what to do with a great idea, examining, among other things, how to evaluate and protect an idea, how to create a business plan, how to structure a business, how to find financing, and how actually to start up a business. This chapter is a distillation of interviews with scores of entrepreneurs, business consultants, attorneys, accountants, and others in related fields.

Part Two concludes with a journal I have kept. This journal provides a firsthand look at the day-to-day ups and downs of following through on an idea. My wife and I did not start a "Postpartum" clothing line. We convinced ourselves that we were too involved at home and at work to start anything new. But, during the course of researching and writing this book, I woke up with another exciting idea. Perhaps inspired by the fun and success enjoyed by the entrepreneurs I was interviewing, I decided to make that idea into a reality. I quickly found myself on an emotional rollercoaster and began to keep the journal so that I might convey those ups and downs to those of you who are thinking about taking a similar journey.

As my journal and the profiles of the successful innovators indicate, the journey is not only exciting. More often than not, it is both emotionally and physically draining. At times, the odds against success may even appear overwhelming. To ignore the possibility of failure is unreasonable. But, as George Bernard Shaw once noted, all progress is made by unreasonable people.

The innovators in this book *do* put their pants on one leg at a time and are the first to admit that they are ordinary people. I hope that their experiences and the other information provided here inspire you to enjoy both the vitality of thought and the pleasure of living beyond your means.

2

Guardian Angels and Business Angles: Creating and Selling a Product

---

To be creative, you have to be an optimist. To be a businessman, you have to be a realist.
— KIP FULLER

If you are a creative optimist with a great idea for a product, you have two basic options. You can either go into business and sell the product, or you can try to sell your *idea* for the product to an existing business. (See profile of Marvin Rosenblum, Chapter 4, and Chapter 9, page 153). Sometimes, even if you had planned to sell the idea, you may end up in business. This chapter profiles entrepreneurs who have started such businesses, in more than one case, quite by accident. Each of these profiles considers different aspects of production, marketing, and distribution. Ann and Mike Moore are dedicated parents who designed, produced, and even retailed a product that, after going relatively unnoticed for more than a decade, "suddenly" revolutionized parenting. Kip Fuller is a professional inventor whose idea for a party gimmick turned into one of the biggest retail hits of the Christmas season. And Leland Wilkinson is a professor who, unable to satisfactorily sell his idea for a software program, went into business.

ANN AND MIKE MOORE
– SNUGLI, INC. –

Necessity is not always the mother of invention. In the case of America's preeminent infant carrier, for example, the mother of invention was, er, a mother. Ann Moore gave birth to the carrier, christened Snugli, at the same time she gave birth to her first daugher, Mande. Today, over twenty years later, both Mande and Snugli have grown up. Originally conceived as an item for Ann's personal use only, not for sale, the Snugli has evolved into a highly popular, mass-merchandised product. Annual sales now exceed $5 million in the United States, and distributors and licensees sell the carriers worldwide.

This is not an overnight success story. When the Snugli arrived, "parenting" was not yet a verb, much less a movement. And natural childbirth and breastfeeding were still a decade away from general acceptance. The Snugli was, in effect, a product whose time had not yet come. It survived only because of the parentlike devotion of its creators, and, says Ann's husband Mike, "Because we had a guardian angel."

Regrettably, this book offers no advice on the supernatural aspects of entrepreneurship. The reader is left to his or her own devices to find guardian angels and the like. Still, the down-to-earth story of the Snugli's evolution and the company's growth is fascinating. Moreover, it presents almost every issue involved when an innovator attempts to sell his or her product.

The Idea and the Prototype

Ann Moore was not thinking about designing something to take to market when she came up with the idea for the Snugli. Rather, she was thinking about designing something in which she could take her baby to *the* market. Searching for a practical and loving way to keep Mande close to her, Ann recalled something she had observed during Peace Corps service in Togo, West Africa. "In the noisy marketplace there, we discovered the marvelous inner calm of the African mothers and their children," she says. "We didn't hear any babies crying, and we saw that the children were being held with long shawls snugly against their mothers' backs while the women worked."

When Mande Moore was born in 1964, infant carriers had not yet been introduced in the American marketplace. Recognizing that she herself was incapable of producing a carrier, Ann did what every innovator in a similar position should do: she found someone with the skills necessary to create the product. That "someone" was her mother, Lucy Aukerman, a skilled needleworker. Mother and daughter stayed up all night designing and creating what they thought would be the first and only carrier. "It was not an idea for a business," says Mike. "It was a means to better parenting. We had no thought of marketing it."

A Market "Survey"

Ann Moore wore daughter and carrier (it did not have a name then) strapped across her front almost everywhere she went. Mande attracted a great deal of attention, and so, too, did the carrier, in effect a corduroy pouch with openings for the baby's head, arms, and legs. Almost immediately, friends, neighbors, and others in the Dayton, Ohio area in which the Moores then lived began to ask where they could get such a carrier. Without knowing it, the Moores were conducting a market survey of the product. The response of the community indicated there was a desire, if not a need, for the carrier. When people began to ask Ann Moore to make carriers for them, the Moores had a decision to make.

Going into Business

Mike Moore was no stranger to the business world. As an undergraduate at Yale, he had demonstrated entrepreneurial prowess by beginning a successful used-furniture operation. But after college, he and Ann had devoted themselves to work in community-based poverty and civil rights programs. Occupied with this work and now beginning a family, the couple had to determine if they had the desire to sell carriers, even on a limited basis. They also had to determine if they had the means for making them, namely if Ann's mother would sew.

"Ann eventually agreed to make someone else a Snugli because she loved what the product stood for," says Mike. "And Lucy went along because she loved to sew. Obviously you're not going to make one for somebody and lose money on it." The Moores were in business.

During its early years, this business was decidedly a ma and pa and grandma operation. Ann took orders for the product; Mike did the books on the weekend; and Lucy, back home in the traditional Dunkard (German Baptist) farming community of West Alexandria, Ohio, made the carriers. There was minimal financial risk because it was a cash-and-carrier operation. Translation: The product was only made after an order had been received; the business was being financed out of its cash flow.

But, as orders were not being solicited — there was no advertising, promotion, or attempt to interest retail establishments — there was minimal financial gain as well. About ten carriers were sold per month. More an avocation than a vocation at this stage, the business was structured as that most simple of forms, a sole proprietorship.

The First Marketing Plan, Pricing, and Protection

By the middle 1960s, the Moores had moved to the Denver area, where Mike directed community poverty programs. Carrier sales were beginning to increase, due in part to an unsophisticated but clever new marketing plan. Explains Mike: "We knew that people who ordered from us had either seen Ann or someone else with the carrier, so we determined that there was a natural sales force out there: the purchasers. From that point on, accompanying every carrier that went out was an invitation to become a sales representative." Interested purchasers were sent a card, which when sent in with a new order they had solicited entitled them to a $5 commission. Eventually about 20 percent of the purchasers participated, selling an average of four Snuglis a year. "It had a nice pyramiding effect," says Mike. (The decision to include a note to the purchaser illustrates a basic principle of the mail-order business: it is often wise to send material — a sales invitation, an updated product listing, a reorder form — along with the product itself. By sending it in this manner, the cost of an additional mailing is avoided and the purchaser's attention is virtually guaranteed.)

As sales gradually increased, the Moores determined that the business warranted a greater degree of professionalism. They therefore sought counsel from local experts — an accountant and a patent attorney. Through work in the poverty program, Mike had made the acquaintance of an accountant from the prominent firm of Arthur Anderson & Co. They now met to discuss the pricing of the carrier. Says Moore: "He walked me through how you price a product, how you figure overhead and indirect expenses, what kind of profit margins to have." The carrier had been selling for $20, but the accountant's calculations suggested that $28 was a more fitting price. The price was thus raised 40 percent. That there was no dropoff in sales suggests that had he consulted an accountant even earlier in the process, Mike might have been able to charge $8 more per Snugli from the beginning.

While still in Dayton, the Moores *had* consulted a patent attorney. Unfortunately, instead of asking friends or business acquaintances to recommend a lawyer, they had let their fingers do the walking. The Yellow Pages may be the place to find patent leather shoes, but it is not the place to find a patent attorney. The application for a patent was denied.

In Denver, the Moores were referred by knowledgeable friends to a respected patent attorney, and a patent was eventually secured. The cost for such legal services (remember, this was the middle 1960s) was about $2,000. To the extent that the cash flow of the operation could not cover this sum, the Moores paid for it out of their own pockets.

About this same time, they finally settled on the name Snugli. Why? "We liked the name Womberroom," Mike says with a laugh, "but we didn't think that would fly in Lucy's Dunkard community. Then, we thought of Snuggler, but that was rejected as too generic. Finally, we hit on Snugli, and it was accepted." (This accepting and rejecting was being done by the Patent and Trademark Office in Washington, D.C. It is with this office that the entrepreneur wishing to protect a trade name or symbol must register. A filing fee is required. A search of existing names can save time and money. Attorneys and other specialists will conduct such a search for a fee.)

Production and Distribution

When the Moores moved from Ohio to Colorado, they left behind Lucy Aukerman — mother, grandmother, and Snugli maker. As demand for the Snugli had increased, Lucy had engaged the services of other talented needleworkers in the Dunkard community to help with production. While in Dayton, Mike had taken responsibility for supervising this production and ordering the material necessary to make the carriers. Half a continent away now, he continued in this role. Distance was not a problem. "The telephone is a wonderful device," Mike explains. In other words, the "manufacturer" maintained constant communication with his "factory" (an important lesson for all would-be entrepreneurs).

Here is how production and distribution worked: In Colorado, Ann processed orders for the Snugli. These orders were then mailed or telephoned to Lucy. Lucy then made or arranged for the making of the ordered Snuglis. Lucy also handled the shipping of the completed Snuglis with the sales invitation. When Lucy needed more material to make the Snuglis, she would notify Mike, who would order it and have it shipped directly to her. Mike had found sources for such material at the Denver Public Library. "I haunted that place and found all sorts of great information," he says. His principle source was the *Thomas Register of American Manufacturers,* an encyclopedia of vendors and suppliers of industrial products. "It's wonderful," he says. "Lucy knew what she wanted. I'd look up, say, 'corduroy' in the *Register,* then shotgun letters out to manufacturers asking for a sample swatch, price quotation, and information about the minimum quantity you had to order."

Guardian Angel #1

If there is a common thread that runs through the stories of most successful entrepreneurs it is this: at some point along the road, forces beyond the innovator's control conspired to push the operation to greater heights. Mike Moore insists that in the case of the Snugli, a guardian angel seems to appear whenever a boost is needed.

This angel appeared for the first time in 1967, when, unbeknownst to the Moores, an article praising the Snugli appeared in the periodical version of the then-popular *Whole Earth Catalog*. Sales instantly doubled to about twenty-five per month and soon had increased to thirty or forty per month. The skeptic might argue that such good fortune was not heaven-sent, but that a truly great idea will inevitably capture the hearts and wallets of the public. In any case, the Moores were savvy enough to try to capitalize on the article (as they capitalized on each visit of the "angel").

A New Marketing Plan

In 1968, Mike resigned from his job in the poverty program to become head of the foundation arm of a public-minded Denver corporation. Before this new job began, the entire Moore family headed east on a journey that was part vacation, part business. Bolstered by the *Whole Earth*'s recognition, Mike and Ann sought the whole retail community's involvement. "We went on a mission of parenting, telling every kind of store imaginable how important the Snugli was," Mike says. The result? "We were so convincing, because we really believed what we were saying, that nobody refused us. Everyone ordered." Snugli was now a direct mail *and* wholesaling operation.

If all had gone according to the Moores' script, the story might end here, with the postscript that the retailers had great success and soon Snuglis were in demand around the nation. Frequently, however, the zeal of the missionary manufacturer is lost by the time a product reaches the shelf. If the Moores had been able to stand behind the counter in each store and talk directly to consumers, they undoubtedly would have been able to sell Snuglis. But they had duties in Denver. As it was, the responsibility fell to the store owners, who, naturally, were not as fanatical as the creators and had numerous other products to sell (many, no doubt, produced by entrepreneurs like the Moores). The result? Says Mike, "When we called the stores back to see how they'd done and if they wanted more every one told us nobody had bought."

The Watershed: From Part-Time to Full-Time

While the Snugli languished in the retail outlets, it flourished as a mail-order item. By 1972, sales had reached 300 per month. Of course, such demand, while welcome, was not without its problems. "Ann and her friends were doing fine processing the orders, and Lucy kept up by finding more and more friends to help," says Mike. "But the areas where I was responsible, bookkeeping and production, were really out of control."

Mike's accountant friend had referred him to a smaller and less expensive local accounting service. This service did the business's books monthly and took care of tax reports. Still, Mike found himself swamped with related paperwork that took more and more of his time. Consumed with such paperwork, he had little time to think about other aspects of the business, much less plan for the future.

After almost eight years as a part-time operation, the business had reached a watershed. "Our sales were a hundred thousand dollars a year," says Mike. "It just wasn't fair to treat it as a hobby anymore. Ann and Lucy were holding up their ends. I decided I had to treat things more seriously."

Mike resigned from his job at the foundation. This seems rather drastic, but, he explains, "I was ready to move on anyway. I usually only stayed a few years at any one job, and I had accomplished my goals there."

His new goals were to work twenty hours per week on Snugli business and twenty hours on a new consulting business. Soon, however, Snugli was taking all of his time. "That's what happens to an entrepreneur who is working for himself and loves what he's doing," he says. "Twenty hours turned to sixty hours a week. But I was hooked."

Among Mike's first tasks was the professionalization of the business. Consultations with attorneys and accountants resulted in the change, partially for tax purposes and partially for protection, from sole proprietorship to corporation. (The Moores retained all the stock in the newly structured operation.) For the first time, too, capital was sought from outside sources. Mike approached a bank for a loan of several thousand dollars, for both expansion and day-to-day operation of the business. The bank eventually loaned the money, but only after a well-to-do friend of the Moores pledged a like amount as a sign of faith in the operation and its operators.

While the financial status of the business was of great concern to Mike, so, too, was the financial status of the family. He had resigned from the foundation with the knowledge that he had three months' termination pay due, but soon that money was absorbed. Snugli, Inc., while growing, was not generating the income that his previous job had; the family's income had been reduced by two-thirds. Did he think of returning to the world of steady paychecks? His response echoes the sentiments of most entrepreneurs: "It never entered my mind. I'd had such a taste of freedom working for myself that wild horses couldn't drag me away," he says, then adds, "Besides, we really felt we had a mission to transform parenting attitudes. That fit together with our background of doing things for the betterment of society. We were so secure philosophically that the financial cuts were not hard to take in our heads. We just pulled in our belts and prepared to give it as long as necessary."

Guardian Angel #2

The belts were definitely getting tighter when the guardian angel paid a return visit. Mike had just finished telling Ann that he wasn't sure how they were going to be able to pay the mortgage and feed the children, when a letter arrived from the Blue Ridge–Potomac La Leche League. While the La Leche League is today a well-known organization and would hardly be deemed "radical," it was viewed with a fair amount of suspicion and skepticism in 1972. Not by the Moores, however, who found the League's philosophy (that breast-feeding made babies healthier both physically and psychologically) consistent with their own. The correspondence excited Mike. "It was a love letter," he says. "They told us how much they liked the Snugli and inquired about being able to sell it to mothers and make a profit."

Mike wrote back that the commission system established several years earlier was still in effect. The League wrote back that it knew about the commission, but was more interested in buying Snuglis wholesale. "There was the guardian angel again," says Mike.

Again, the wise entrepreneur is the one who takes advantage of "guardian angels." Despite the Moores' precarious financial position, Mike immediately flew to Washington, D.C., to meet with the League. "My intuition told me this was important," he says.

The meeting was a success, "a love-in," says Mike. Mothers with Snuglis sang the praises of the product, then sat down to talk business. "My original session with the accountant had left a margin to wholesale the product," says Mike. The La Leche League agreed to buy in minimum lots of a dozen. Snugli, Inc. was now, in part at least, a wholesaler.

A Second Marketing Plan

The Blue Ridge–Potomac La Leche League directed Mike to several more groups in the District of Columbia area. Mike sensed that something important was happening, that there was a blossoming network of parenting organizations — La Leche, Lamaze, and others. He called Ann back in Colorado and told her that he was going to stay east and meet with all the groups between Washington, D.C., and Boston. "Two weeks later, I had only gotten as far as Philadelphia," he remembers. "There were so many groups! And therein lay our marketing plan for the next three years."

The plan: market directly to the audience that in the early 1970s was quietly challenging traditional notions of parenthood. "There was a continuum," Mike explains. "Natural childbirth, breastfeeding, and then the Snugli to bond with the child. Parents who saw it realized intuitively that this was right for them." Mike and Ann spent much of the next three years, 1972–1975, in a station wagon, crisscrossing the country to call on these parents and their organizations. Recognizing that there was a danger of neglecting their own parental responsibilities — there were now three little Moores — they took the children along whenever possible.

Advertising

A station wagon can only cover so much ground. Aware that a growing audience for the Snugli now existed and that they could not personally reach every member of that audience, the Moores for the first time entered the world of advertising. "We went about it in a professional way," Mike explains. A top media specialist was engaged and a plan developed. They would zero in on magazines catering to their targeted audience.

Parents Magazine seemed a natural outlet in which to kick off the campaign. Like many entrepreneurs, Mike was surprised by the cost of taking out an advertisement. "Holy mackerel!" he says. "It was expensive. It cost something like six thousand dollars." The result: "I think we sold six," Mike says. "We got burned. We stayed away from advertising for a long time after that."

Mike is at loss to explain why the advertising effort failed, just as he is at a loss to explain why the stores approached several years earlier failed to sell any Snuglis. There is a lesson here: Even the most successful entrepreneurs do not score with every decision, every campaign. Some plans work (direct marketing to parents' organizations); some plans do not work (advertising). But as long as the entire business is not being risked on such experiments, it can probably survive so that other approaches can be tried or the same experiment can be conducted at a later date. The Moores risked $6,000 on the advertising effort. The loss of that money hurt, but was hardly fatal. On the other hand, if they had risked tens of thousands of dollars on their first flirtation with this new and unknown medium of advertising, the business might have been in trouble.

Guardian Angel #3

In 1971, prior to contact with the La Leche League, retail mail-order sales to individuals constituted 95 percent of the Snugli business; wholesale sales to stores accounted for the remainder. By 1975, mail-order sales constituted only 10 percent of the business; a full 60 percent of sales were to parenting organizations, while stores accounted for the remaining 30 percent.

The business was thriving, but to reach an even greater audience (and greater profits) greater distribution in retail establishments was required. To attract such outlets, the Moores had begun to visit trade shows, in particular the Juvenile Products show. Their success at these shows had been limited. Enter guardian angel number three.

In October 1975, the influential magazine *Consumer Reports* reviewed soft and frame baby carriers. The magazine concluded that among the half-dozen or so soft carriers, Snugli was the best. (Again, the guardian angel would have been of little value if the product had not been superior.) "The results were astounding," says Mike. "When we showed up at the next show, the manufacturers' reps and stores came at us like gangbusters." Sales jumped like gangbusters, too. By 1978, Lucy Aukerman and friends were producing 8,000 Snuglis a month. Ninety-five percent of these were being wholesaled to retail outlets.

Centuries after the women of Togo, West Africa, had designed their baby carriers, fourteen years after Ann Moore had conceived of the first Snugli, the American business world and general public had caught on to the product and the values it embodied. Ann Moore has no regrets that it took a decade and a half to become "an overnight sensation." Says Ann: "The belt-tightening was good. We had a long time to lay a foundation."

Distribution and Production

Demand for a product is relatively worthless if it cannot be satisfied. The Moores were faced with the task of ensuring that stores were able to buy all the Snuglis the public was demanding. Selling directly to retailers at trade shows was not enough. The Moores employed sales representatives to visit stores around the country and sell the Snugli. As the actions of sales representatives reflect directly upon the companies they are representing, the Moores were careful about whom they hired. The Snugli was still a relatively new concept, so it was important that the representatives understood the values it embodied and, of course, how it worked. Ann trained the representatives on both these scores, and the reps in turn educated the retailers to whom they sold the product.

Increased demand raised another issue. Explains Mike: "We had to figure out how to make them fast enough and ship them fast enough to the stores." The number of cottages in the industry under Lucy's supervision had grown to 150, stretching from Dayton to Richmond, Indiana. More were needed. "It was like an eighteen-wheel semi careening down a winding mountain road," says Mike. "It seemed like it was out of control, but somehow it made it."

Unwilling to try the road too many times, the Moores reached a critical conclusion. "We figured if we could mass-produce, then we could make a lot more than eight thousand per month. That made a lot more sense than trying to find more cottage workers," says Mike.

It also made sense to try to produce a version of the Snugli that would be affordable to an even larger portion of the public. Up to this point, Snuglis had been made out of corduroy or seersucker. Lucy now designed a new, less costly version out of denim. It was christened "Snugli 2." Often entrepreneurs with a prototype must find someone who can ensure that the prototype can be mass-produced. By word of mouth, Mike found an industrial engineer who had a specialty in the needle industry to engineer a factory form for just that purpose.

A Factory: Finding a Site, Financing, and Work Force

Now all that was needed was a factory. Finding a site for the factory was not difficult. A large dog kennel on the land neighboring their lovely wooded home outside Denver turned out to be perfectly suitable. Finding financing was another matter. When business had boomed, Mike had hired an accountant friend to work full-time on the company's finances. Together they calculated that $500,000 — substantially more than the business could provide out of its cash flow — would be required for the purchase and renovation of the kennel into corporate headquarters and operating factory. They presented a comprehensive plan to a local bank, which in turn proposed a loan guaranteed by the Small Business Administration (SBA). The loan was eventually approved, and Snugli 2's were soon rolling off the assembly line. The economics of this system made a great deal of sense to Snugli, Inc. The Snuglis were wholesaled to stores at two-thirds the cost of the original Snugli (which was still being custom-made in Ohio), but retailed for only one-half the cost because the stores took a lower markup.

Finding a site and financing were relatively easy compared to finding a good work force. Initially, the assembly line operation was plagued with absenteeism and high employee turnover. Soon, however, the company had tapped into Denver's growing Southeast Asian refugee community, a gold mine of reliable and talented workers.

Growth and Expansion

A smooth factory operation opened up many new avenues to the company. Explains Mike: "In the past we hadn't gone after the catalogs, showrooms, and mass merchandisers because we'd been scared that our cottage industry couldn't have met their demand. If Sears orders half a dozen Snuglis for each store, that's a lot of Snuglis." Now these huge outlets could be considered. So, too, could foreign markets. Snugli, Inc., was soon supplying Sears and similar firms in the United States and working out licensing and distribution arrangements outside the country.

Postscript

Snugli, Inc., is no longer a small, part-time business, and it is no longer a new business. Mande Moore is twenty-one years old now. So is the company. Annual sales are in the neighborhood of $5 million. The problems of generating awareness and demand have been replaced by the problems of dealing with unions and the effect of a strong dollar on overseas operations. The managerial staff has expanded. The company is still closely held, but the Moores no longer hold all the stock in the corporation. New products have been added, and much of the factory work is now being done overseas, then shipped to the United States for sale. "We're in the major leagues now," admits Mike.

At what point the next guardian angel will make an appearance is anybody's guess. Periodically, larger companies have approached the Moores about buying the entire operation. Mike insists he is interested only in selling Snuglis, not Snugli, Inc. With true entrepreneurial spirit, he explains, "It's too much fun running the thing."

LESSONS FROM ANN AND MIKE MOORE

1. If you have an idea that you think is better, have confidence in it. Dare to try. Don't just dream about it.
2. Understand your own limitations. Always turn to people who are better than you are at what you are trying to solve and get their input, whether it's graphic design, industrial engineering, or whatever.
3. Follow your intuition.
4. Have fun. You have to love what you are doing.

KIP FULLER
– SERVITRON ROBOTS, INC. –

Whereas Ann and Mike Moore are not professional inventors, Kip Fuller is. Whereas the Moore's Snugli is not a high-technology item, Fuller's Servitron Robot is. And whereas the Moores introduced the Snugli slowly, with little capital and even less promotion, Fuller introduced the robot with a great deal of capital and even greater promotion. Fuller, however, does share some similarities with the Moores. He, too, is based in the Denver area, and, more important, he, too, has been highly successful. In just its first full year of operation, Servitron Robot's sales approached $2 million. Finally, Fuller's story, like that of the Moores, presents important insights into the creation, marketing, and sale of a new product.

Starting Out

"I wasn't a natural inventor," says Kip Fuller. "I wasn't able to put puzzles together. I'd come up with ideas, but they'd usually be shot down." When he did try to build things, the results were not always rosy. One of his first creations was a fiberglass expansion chamber designed to increase the oomph of the motorcycle he raced. It exploded. Fuller was still a teenager at the time.

A few years later, at age twenty-two, Fuller invented his first product that could be sold to the public. The TricTrailer was a folding utility trailer that attached to a car for hauling boats, motorcycles, and other items. With visions of glory, Fuller and a childhood friend, Gary Schlatter, went into business. Only after moving into an impressive office, hiring several employees, and selling some 3,000 of the trailers did the pair realize they were losing $25 on each sale. "You can't make that up with volume," Schlatter later told a newspaper. The humor of the situation was lost on Fuller, who claims, "It was the first time I ever failed at anything. I'd always succeeded at school, in sports, with women."

Fuller and Schlatter, now in their early thirties, are still partners. Fuller invents and helps with the marketing of new products, while Schlatter is responsible for finances and the day-to-day operations of their various ventures. "We're a good pair," says Fuller. "We move in different lanes on the highway. Gary's my safety net. He'll come up behind me and say, 'This isn't consistent.'"

Since the TricTrailer, the partners have enjoyed consistent success. Fuller's last two inventions to reach the market have done extremely well. The first is the popular Aqua Tunes. A sort of Snugli for the swim set, Aqua Tunes is a waterproof pouch with earphones for people who want to listen to their portable radios and cassette players while they swim. A variation of Aqua Tunes, Aqua Coach, went to the 1984 Summer Olympics. This device allowed two-way radio communication between water-sports competitors and their coaches. The second successful invention is the Servitron Robot, a four-foot-high, inflatable creature which can be dressed as a maid, chef, or butler. Radio-controlled by a hand-held transmitter, the robot can serve cocktails and hors d'oeuvres at a distance of up to seventy-five feet and can move forward, move in reverse, and turn. But perhaps its most appealing feature is its price: It retails for less than $100.

The Idea and the Prototype

The robot was born Christmas, 1983. Fuller and Schlatter throw a formal Christmas party for their clients every year. That Christmas, they could not afford to cater the party (no matter how successful they are, full-time inventors seem to have constant cash flow problems). Fuller, never intending to sell robots, designed a prototype merely to take the place of the human caterers and entertain the partygoers.

A Market "Survey"

In a sense, the story of the robot here parallels the story of the Snugli. Just as people on the street asked Ann Moore where to get an infant carrier, people at the party asked Fuller and Schlatter where they could get the robots. Fuller is not generally impressed by such idle chatter. A long time member of the put-your-money-where-your-mouth-is school, he finds many first-time inventors all too anxious to sink money into production after the first relative or friend raves about an idea. He therefore advises all budding entrepreneurs to see how serious such boosters are by asking them to write checks. At the Christmas party such solicitation was turned over to the robot itself; a sign hung hastily around its neck encouraged the impressed to buy immediately. "There were about two hundred and fifty people at the party, and about fifty of them wrote checks on the spot," says Fuller. "We knew we had something." The next step was determining whether the retailers agreed. Their plan was to attract a major retailer and then, with that retailer's endorsement in hand, attract financing.

Marketing the Product

Both Fuller and Schlatter have backgrounds in marketing. Their experience convinced them that the robot should, initially at least, be sold through prestigious retail outlets. They viewed the robot as a toy for the well-to-do. One store in particular appealed to them: Neiman-Marcus.

Should an entrepreneur begin by pitching a new product at the top of the retail pyramid? Or is it wiser to start a little lower, testing the sales pitch on an establishment whose participation is not essential? Fuller and Schlatter opted for the top. Explains Fuller, "We figured we'd come this far, we might as well start with our first choice first. If they say no, at least you have a chance with the other outlets."

Some retailers refuse to consider products from parties with whom they have never done business — which makes it hard for new parties wishing to enter new markets. Some retailers only consider products which have already been successful in other stores; this is frequently the case with mass merchandisers, who prefer to see a new item prove itself in, say, specialty shops. Fortunately for the Kip Fullers of the world, some retailers will consider unproven products from unknown innovators. Neiman-Marcus, known for its unique items, falls into this final category.

Fuller called Neiman-Marcus to find the name of the buyer who would be responsible for purchasing robots. Soon that buyer received an eight-by-ten photo of the robot and a slick packet that Fuller describes as "similar to a press release." The packet extolled the virtues of the robot and also presented Servitron Robot's marketing strategy: that adults *need* toys.

The price of a product will influence a retailer quite a bit. The suggested retail price for this toy was under $100. Fuller was confident that Neiman-Marcus would be impressed by the robot itself, but feared the retailer might think it was not expensive enough to generate a good profit. To nip this problem in the bud, he offered the robot at a low wholesale rate that allowed a high margin of profit for the store.

Shortly after sending the letter to Neiman-Marcus, Fuller followed up with a phone call. The news was good. Neiman-Marcus wanted to meet the robot. Fuller planned for this meeting very carefully. He wanted to leave as little to chance as possible. The result was a dramatic performance by both man and machine.

Selling the Buyer

Fuller did not want the fate of the robot to be determined by a buyer sitting alone in a back room. "Buyers don't like to make decisions," he explains. He decided, therefore, to flush the buyer out and make the decision for her. "I made the robot give our presentation," he says. "I entered the office, didn't tell the receptionist who I was, and just started the robot. I knew it would put the whole office in stitches, and it did. I created some excitement. Everyone was running around calling for the buyer, saying she had to see this." By the time the buyer did come, her fellow workers had made the decision for her. They insisted she take the robot for Neiman-Marcus.

The robot, then, literally sold itself. "It's not often you have a chance to sell like this," Fuller says. "But when you do, you should take advantage of it."

Finding Financing

While Neiman-Marcus's response reinforced Fuller's feeling that he "had something," he also knew he did not have something else: the $800,000 necessary to finance the large-scale operation he and Schlatter envisioned. They wanted to enter the market, as Fuller says, "guns blazing," because they believed that such an entrance would discourage competition.

Fuller and Schlatter's resources were insufficient to either directly support the proposed venture or secure a bank loan for it. They therefore sought financial help from outside investors. Here, they found they had to walk a fine line. They wanted money from investors, but not advice. Says Fuller, "It's dangerous to give up the company to people who do not do this kind of thing day in and day out. If an oil man is investing money in a product related to his field, that's fine. But if it's new products, he's squeamish. He may be optimistic in the beginning, but it doesn't last. You don't want those kinds of hands in there."

The hands Fuller eventually found belonged to two wealthy real estate people who were willing to take a large piece of the financial pie in return for staying out of the kitchen. They cosigned the loan from the bank and received a 50 percent share of profits, a $70,000 initiation fee, and interest. Fuller admits the price was high, but argues that the new business was able to establish a sophisticated supply and distribution system from the beginning of operation. This ensured immediate credibility with the national accounts they sought; if a retailer does not believe a manufacturer can supply the product in the quantity and manner desired, the odds are the retailer will not order the product — no matter how wonderful it may be.

Manufacturing the Product

The Servitron Robot consists of several components. Initially Fuller ordered these components from Asian manufacturers found in a guide similar to the *Thomas Register*. The robots were assembled at Fuller's Denver headquarters until the design was perfected. After that, Fuller found an Asian company to assemble the robots.

Postscript

A number of similar establishments soon joined Neiman-Marcus in selling the robot. Retailing in the stores and their catalogs for less than $100, the product was one of the major successes of the 1984 Christmas season. In its first full year of operation Servitron sold 50,000 of the robots and the company's sales totaled approximately $2 million. Fuller and Schlatter could afford human caterers for their 1984 Christmas party. Second-year sales were nearly double those of the first, and the robot soon had a best friend. The friend, marketed as The Space Mutt, is a robot that looks like a dog. It has fur, but it, too, is inflatable. Fuller notes that it has one big advantage over real dogs: "It only drops batteries on the floor."

The Key: An Educated Public

Fuller notes two reasons for the dramatic success of the robot. The first is apparent: "It was affordable," he says. The second is more subtle. "The public was already educated for something like this."

Fuller thinks twice about going forward with a new invention if, as he says, "you have to tell someone what it does twice. Any product like that, look out! But if you can put it in front of him and *he'll* tell *you* what it does, then you may have something." In a sense, the Snugli, as simple as it was in design, was introduced to an uneducated public. That is, no doubt, a major reason it took so long to reach the same stores the robot reached so quickly. Movies like *Star Wars* and years of talk about robots had created a climate in which few people had to ask what the creature did.

Had he designed something like the Snugli before the revolution in parenting, Fuller would probably have put it in the office closet he calls the rubber room. There, awaiting an educated public, sit a number of inventions, including a device that releases ski boot bindings when a skier falls and ski pants with built-in knee braces. Fuller will wait to introduce these until the time is right and the public clamors for new ideas in ski safety.

The time is right, he believes, for his most recent (and most sobering) invention: the Guardian Alcohol Ignition System. Having designed a robot that serves drinks, Fuller has now designed a system that prevents a person who has had too many drinks from starting a car. An automobile fitted with the Guardian may not be started without first breath-testing the operator's blood alcohol level. The device can be installed by any car radio installation center and sells for under $500 installed. Fuller's marketing strategy for the product is inspired. He is working with court systems to offer installation of the Guardian as an alternative to license suspension for first-time drunk-driving offenders.

Fuller on the Guardian recalls the Moores on the Snugli. There is something almost evangelical about his tone. "It's nice when something you invent can be of such benefit to society," he says. "I'm not playing anymore."

LESSONS FROM
KIP FULLER

1. Ask yourself the hard question. Does my product have an appeal, and what is that appeal? Don't cheat when answering.
2. Decide whether this is a business or a hobby. If you decide it is a business, you had better get people around you who are good at the things you aren't good at.
3. This is a young person's, a young single person's game. You're going to take your family with you the first few times, and you may lose them. If you're not prepared to do that, wait until your dependents are grown and you can take the risk. We almost have to have a company policy that employees cannot have girlfriends or boyfriends. If a relationship backfires, it can hurt a project. It's too competitive out there to let that happen.
4. If you have a business which specializes in new products, the key is diversity. You want a mix of products that cycle quickly and long term, stable products.
5. You have a year to apply for a patent. It's a big waste to spend the money and go after it right away. Don't consult a patent attorney until you see there is a market, until you see if people are willing to write you a check. Your money, particularly at the beginning, may be better spent on marketing. Marketing is much more important than a patent.
6. If you do go to a patent attorney, ask what the chances for success are. Don't take "I'm not sure," for an answer. It's an escape for an attorney to say, "I don't know. I'm not a businessman." If the attorney can't tell you it's worthwhile, or will only say, "We'll try," then consult two or three more attorneys.

LELAND WILKINSON
– SYSTAT, INC. –

While some innovators have no intention of selling their ideas for new products to an existing business, others may not want to go into business for themselves, choosing instead to sell the great idea itself. As the discussion in Chapter 9 demonstrates, selling an idea is not necessarily the easiest route, or in the case of Leland Wilkinson, the most profitable proposition.

Leland Wilkinson is a deceptive character. He looks young and innocent enough to lead one to the conclusion that very few years have passed since he was last asked to produce identification so he could get a beer. Yet he is actually in his early forties, his oldest daughter already off to college. True, his bookish appearance does not belie his nine-to-five existence; he is a professor of psychology teaching statistics to graduate students at the University of Illinois–Chicago, and he looks the part. But beneath the calculator in his breast pocket, there beats the heart of a man who cannot help taking his BMW well past the speed limit whenever he gets on the highway. "I've almost lost my license for speeding a few times," he says, shaking his head. Then he smiles. "It bothered me until I heard Steven Jobs, the founder of Apple Computers, has the same problem."

If Wilkinson does not project the Mario Andretti image, neither does he suggest Lee Iacocca. He looks too academic to have the moxie to flourish in the business world, particularly the fast-moving world of computer technology. But flourish he has. In less than two years, working part-time, he has built up a software company with gross annual sales exceeding $2 million. And he never intended to go into business!

The Idea and the Prototype

Wilkinson recalls his first computer with fondness. "I built it from a kit," he says proudly. "It took a year, and required 7,168 solders in the memory board alone." Wilkinson did not need the computer to figure out that the cost of sending two bright daughters to college was going to put a financial strain on the family. But he did need a computer to do something about it. Early in 1983, after discussing with his wife Ruth Van Demark how he might generate additional income, Wilkinson decided to create a program that would allow statisticians to do on microcomputers what at the time could only be done on mainframe computers. As a statistician himself, he knew how valuable such a program could be to those in academia, private industry, and government. His plan was simple: on an upcoming sabbatical, he would spend all his spare time designing the program. Then he would sell it to a software manufacturer or publisher and collect a royalty on sales.

If the plan was simple, the execution of it was not. Some months later, Wilkinson found himself sitting dazed after an all-night session with the computer. "I'd been spending so much time on the program that my brain was fried," Wilkinson says. "I couldn't even remember my home phone number." Somehow, he did manage to remember the number of a friend who was expert in matters of neurology. "I asked him if I could get permanent brain damage from what I was doing," says Wilkinson. "He told me to go to bed." Wilkinson complied, but he spent several more sleepless nights before he was able to succeed where those before him had failed. By the fall of 1983, Wilkinson had his prototype package, consisting of the software and a draft of an explanatory manual.

Selling: Part One

The prototype Wilkinson had created was more than just an idea, but less than a finished product. It was, in many ways, like a manuscript which awaits the efforts of editor and publishing house before it becomes a book with a cover, ready for sale to the public. Wilkinson had no intention of publishing the package himself. He had neither time nor distribution network nor business experience to do so. Therefore, he identified the major software publishers in the field and set about interesting them in the package.

A convention of a professional association or a trade association attracts more than just professionals or tradesmen. Vendors who offer products and services to the conventioneers are always present, marketing their wares. Wilkinson knew that the major software publishers in the statistics field would be at the fall gathering of the American Statistical Association, of which he was a member. These publishers were his "target market," and he arranged to show the package to them at the convention. Wilkinson's professional colleagues who saw the program in action were impressed and wanted to buy copies of it. Several companies also expressed interest in publishing and selling the program.

Among the bidders was one of the most prestigious publishers of scientific material. Soon Wilkinson was involved in serious negotiations with this publisher. After several telephone calls, letters, and meetings, the two parties seemed to have reached an understanding. The publisher would pay Wilkinson a $20,000 advance, and then a royalty after sales reached a certain level.

The figure was certainly heady, but a variety of doubts plagued Wilkinson. "The contract was really weighted against me," he says, acknowledging that this seems to be the practice in the industry and deters few from signing. In addition, Wilkinson was not completely happy with the editor assigned to his package. He also wondered how aggressively the publisher would promote the book.

A friend at another company that published software had previously advised him to market the package himself. Wilkinson didn't think he had the time or skills to go into the software business. Now, as he sat in his hotel room in New York preparing to visit the publisher and sign the contract, he was beginning to have second thoughts. Wilkinson's wife, a lawyer, had no second thoughts. "I was opposed to signing," says Ruth Van Demark. So opposed that she called Wilkinson from Chicago at six o'clock on the morning he was to sign and told him "Don't." And thus Wilkinson's fortunes turned at the eleventh hour. He was now, it appeared, in the software business.

Starting Up

Wilkinson's company, Systat, Inc., began full-scale operations early in 1984. With the aid of his brother-in-law, a corporate lawyer, Wilkinson drafted a *pro forma,* a document which projected expenses and revenues. This document, based on the demand evidenced at the

American Statistical Association convention, projected a worst-case scenario of a $20,000 profit in the first year of operation. On the basis of that projection, Wilkinson was able to secure for the business a $15,000 loan from a local bank. He did, however, have to personally guarantee the loan. The money was used to hire an office person–bookkeeper and produce the software and accompanying manual. The company operated out of Wilkinson's basement. "We were pretty unsophisticated," Wilkinson now recalls, smiling. And pretty nervous. "Despite the *pro forma,* I wasn't even sure if we'd break even," he admits.

Selling: Part Two

Wilkinson laughs when he recalls Systat's first marketing effort. "We used the computer to make a seven-page brochure," he says. "But I forgot to number the pages." The brochure, sent to targeted statisticians, generated many calls and some sales, as did a few small advertisements in the magazine *Byte,* the bible of the software industry. "After all that work developing the program, it looked like we were just going to break even," says Wilkinson. During the first three months of operation, approximately eighty programs were sold at $200 a piece. How had Wilkinson determined the price? "It was a wild guess," he admits.

And how did Wilkinson actually "manufacture" his product? He simply used his home computer to copy his program onto blank disks purchased at the local software store that gave him the best price. As for the accompanying instructional manual, "I looked in the Yellow Pages and found a printer," he recalls.

In the meantime, unbeknownst to Wilkinson, the April 1984 issue of *Byte* reviewed statistics software packages. The magazine praised Systat as the best program on the market. "After that the phone didn't stop ringing," says Wilkinson. "We had call waiting, but I think we still only managed to get 10 percent of the calls."

Postscript

A little more than a year after the magazine review that changed his lifestyle, if not life, Leland Wilkinson sits in the offices of Systat, Inc.

No longer a basement operation, the company operates out of modern quarters in a bank building. Wilkinson is surrounded by computers and the desks of several employees. Systat has a full-time business manager now, and a consultant who, along with Wilkinson, answers knotty software problems when they arise. (Wilkinson still teaches part-time.)

Wilkinson is reviewing a full-page, professionally produced Systat advertisement that will appear in a computer magazine at a cost of $10,000. He hardly seems the same person who had to be pushed into going into business, who couldn't remember to number the pages of his promotional literature. He makes all the important decisions at the company. "When this started I thought of myself as a naive academic," he says. "But I'm surprised how canny my business sense has been. People are surprised that when they present me with options I can make a decision so quickly. I kind of have a grab-the-moment philosophy."

For example, "We waited before we spent a lot on marketing," Wilkinson says, noting that several software companies have gone under after devoting most of their resources immediately to advertising. Systat instead spent a great deal of time cultivating its relationships with universities, figuring that the statisticians–Systat users of tomorrow are in the classrooms today.

The White House, Fortune 500 companies, and numerous statisticians worldwide are already using the Systat program. Sales are booming. "In the past I could spend my free time thinking, writing, sailing, just lying in the hammock." Wilkinson sighs. "This has ruined my quiet academic existence."

He doesn't look disappointed.

LESSONS FROM
LELAND WILKINSON

1. Talk to accountants who know what they're doing. I had tax problems because I didn't.
2. Hire people who come recommended by people you trust.

3. Try to create a spirit of camaraderie in the office. It makes work more fun.

The entrepreneurs who have successfully sold ideas and products have blended optimism and realism. Ann and Mike Moore may have been optimistic about the prospects for the Snugli, but they were realistic enough to let the times and the general public catch up with their thinking before they made the endeavor anything more than a hobby. Kip Fuller was realistic enough to realize that if he wanted his robot to succeed he would have to give up a large share of the profits to those who could bankroll the operation. Leland Wilkinson's realistic appraisal of his circumstances allowed him to change course at the eleventh hour and profit from his ideas.

3

From Typesetting to Matchmaking: Creating and Starting a Service

I've always sold my business on the basis of who I am. When I first started, I put my picture on my business card so people knew that I was young and a woman. If you say what you are up front, then you shouldn't have any problems later on.

— JULIE BRUMLIK

Julie Brumlik, founder and president of Scarlett Letters, Inc., a popular typography service in New York City, arrived in New York from Alabama as a teenager with little money. She worked as a typesetter for, among others, Ayn Rand's foundation before striking off on her own. She has kept to the above-described philosophy throughout her career. After Scarlett Letters became a success, Brumlik was approached by the owner of one of Holland's larger typography concerns. He was looking for an American partner. "Our first meeting was scheduled right after my trapeze class," recalls Brumlik, whose other interests including trekking in the Himalayas and flying helicopters. "I considered not going to the class so he wouldn't think I was eccentric. But then it occurred to me, he should know what he was getting into. There was no way I could keep up the deception if we were ever going to work together."

Products often seem to sell themselves. A need arises; a product is created to meet that need; the consumer buys the product. It is in some ways a rather impersonal process. Not so with services. As Julie Brumlik suggests, the proprietor selling a service is really selling herself or himself. A video dating service sounds interesting. But who is running it? Is he honest? Will he exercise good judgment?

In the profiles that follow, innovative individuals have turned ideas for services into successful businesses. In the process, the individuals became synonymous with those services. Julie Brumlik's typesetting business is not a new idea in itself. But the manner in which she has developed the business reflects her unique personality. Jeffrey Ullman's video dating service is, he insists, the logical extension of his own political philosophy.

JULIE BRUMLIK
– SCARLETT LETTERS, INC. –

The Dutchman apparently liked what he saw in Julie Brumlik. A few hours after their initial meeting the pair boarded a plane for Holland, and the next day they signed a brief document creating a multimillion-dollar union. "When I got back to New York, my lawyer wasn't too happy," smiles Brumlik, a frank and engaging, scarlet-haired woman in her middle thirties.

The lawyer was equally miffed a few days later when Brumlik's new partner wired her several hundred thousand dollars. Brumlik added a substantial portion of her own capital, and went out and spent over $1 million on a factory and hi-tech equipment. It was a good investment. Today, Scarlett Letters bills over $2 million annually in New York alone, and some $17 million worldwide.

Such figures do not appear to faze Brumlik, who started the company with $32 in her pocket and a Gimbel's credit card, which she used as a credit reference to secure her original equipment. "Entrepreneurs like money, but they don't care about it like other people," she says. "In fact, they really don't care what business it is that they're in. They like playing the game. And they like having complete control over an idea."

The Idea

It was the desire to control her own destiny and ideas that led Brumlik to begin Scarlett Letters. The cost of renting the basic machinery necessary to operate a small typesetting operation was $200. "I figured even if the typesetting business was slow I could make that much selling newspapers," she says.

The typesetting industry in New York is male-dominated and under the control of second-generation companies that have had years to develop accounts. Brumlik's early clients, therefore, were those whom the establishment did not want: Greenwich Village shop owners in need of signs, small business people in need of business cards, gypsy fortunetellers. "I'd just get on my bike and ride around asking if people needed business," she says. "I tried to get two or three jobs a day, and I had no idea what to charge." This approach — she was literally wheeling and dealing — foreshadowed the way Brumlik was to operate even after Scarlett Letters was well in the black. She was selling herself, her eagerness and enthusiasm, and her offbeat way of looking at things.

Marketing the Service and Herself

Several hundred miles after beginning her bicycle campaign, Brumlik determined she was ready for bigger accounts. Bringing new meaning to the term "networking," she planned a huge party in her small apartment, then passed out invitations to appropriate-looking people she met in stores, bars, and the park. Art directors at advertising agencies, corporations, and publishers were her targets. She wanted them to come and meet her. More than a few showed up at the party, and one eventually hired her to do the typesetting for a medical magazine. "I think they were impressed by my resourcefulness and the fact that I could do it much cheaper," says Brumlik.

Professionalization

The winning of her first major account made it necessary to professionalize the operation. Brumlik, like many young entrepreneurs, had, as she says, "been flying by the seat of my pants." She had not incorporated, nor received accounting or legal advice. She also did not have the staff required to handle the new client. In short order, she found help (a part-time circus clown, who was succeeded by an evangelist); she found a feminist lawyer; and she found an accountant. Says Brumlik: "I hadn't been professional. I was just making a list of jobs and crossing them off when I got paid."

Setting Herself Apart from Competitors

There are over one thousand typography firms in New York City, and a handful of them vie for the lucrative overnight assignments of making up the copy for advertising agencies and magazines. In competing for this business, Brumlik soon came to realize that if she could establish solid relationships with the art directors at these concerns, then her chances of winning and expanding accounts would be greatly improved. The first step toward achieving this is good service. "I worked three shifts a day and weekends," Brumlik says. "I sold what artists wanted, rather than what I wanted to sell."

Brumlik believes the second step toward winning clients is good promotion. Proceeding on the theory that art directors are forgotten beings in the corporate structure, Brumlik embarked upon a campaign to show them that *she* hadn't forgotten about them. Her hope was that the directors then would not forget about her. How did she set herself apart from competitors? She sent finished work back to the art directors with something extra. Freshly baked croissants, scratch-and-sniff cards, chocolates, flowers. The medium varied, but the message was the same: Scarlett Letters cares. Such promotions quickly earned Brumlik a spot in the hearts of her clients and several spots in the feature sections of New York newspapers and magazines. Business flourished, and within a year she had moved out of her tiny apartment-office into a larger apartment-office.

At about this time, Brumlik managed to start a new business as well. Godiva Messenger Service featured blond-tressed maidens delivering packages not on horseback, but on Harley Davidson motorcycles. As expected, this venture created a great deal of publicity, but problems with insurance forced Brumlik and her partners to shut it down after a year. "We didn't make much money, but we had fun and we paid all our bills," Brumlik says.

By this time Scarlett Letters was doing more than just paying its bills. Within two and a half years of start-up, the company was billing $16,000 a month. Expenses were less than $1,000 a month. By 1980, less than a decade after its birth, Scarlett had its rich European uncle. With her own money and that of her Dutch partner, Brumlik bought and renovated a brownstone in New York's SoHo district, creating an office and factory complex with state-of-the-art equipment.

Postscript

Since forming her intercontinental partnership, Brumlik has not rested on her laurels. Indeed, she doesn't seem to have rested at all. She has solidified Scarlett Letters's position by means of creative direct-mail campaigns to art directors and other clients. Example: Recognizing that many directors were, as she was, émigrés from small towns, she sent a postcard photograph showing two somewhat down-and-out gents biding time on Main Street, U.S.A. "We Love you. Call home. 966-3560. Scarlett," read the missive.

At the same time that she has courted the creative types with her creativity, Brumlik has been wooing the establishment types with decidedly establishment behavior. She now straddles the fence with apparent ease. She is the first woman to be named an officer of the highly traditional Typographers' Association of New York.

While Scarlett Letters now earns praise for its work, it is also hailed as a first-rate place for workers. Brumlik encourages employees to be as active and physical as she is, and the company rents local squash courts, pays for squash lessons, and foots the bill for work-related classes. Informal day care is also provided at the office.

Brumlik's many-colored business card describes her as "Boss" of Scarlett Letters, with offices in New York and eight European and

South American cities. Recently she has embarked on other ventures as well. She is a founder of the new gallery, Art and Industry, which features furniture created by prominent artists, and she is publishing a magazine for those in the graphics business. Brumlik seems to thrive on such busyness and does not worry about being spread too thin. "An entrepreneur is someone who doesn't have to be talked into business," she smiles. "Two or three projects isn't nearly enough."

LESSONS FROM
JULIE BRUMLIK

1. Have confidence in yourself and your ideas.
2. Only do business with people you like.
3. Use direct mail. I have 7,000 names on my list now. Write down the names of the people you meet who may be at all useful, and send them regular mailings. Keep a consistent idea of your customer in your head. I have a picture of the typical art director — where he goes, how he parties, dresses, etc.
4. Don't try to talk people into jobs.
5. Maintain a reputation for integrity.
6. Cultivate the trade associations.
7. Don't get disorganized.
8. Don't worry about someone else's timetable.
9. Be willing to support yourself.
10. Keep a notebook in every pocket. Always be prepared to jot down ideas.

JEFFREY ULLMAN
– GREAT EXPECTATIONS, INC. –

Sometimes great ideas grow out of ideology. A case in point: Los Angeles–based Great Expectations, the nation's first video dating service. Creator and president Jeffrey Ullman insists that the roots of the successful business he started in 1976 can be traced to the political activism of the previous decade. "Power to the People" was the slogan then and remains Ullman's credo to this day. "One of the big differences between our service and most of the others is that we don't matchmake," Ullman says. "We let the client decide."

Ullman's politics can be traced to his days as an undergraduate at the University of California at Berkeley in the late 1960s. "I was extremely active in left-wing politics," Ullman says. Having grown up in Los Angeles during the birth of the television era, Ullman had always been sensitive to the power of TV. At Berkeley, he came to appreciate the political implications of the medium. "Look at Vietnam," he says. "Television was a tool by which clever politicians communicated messages, ideas, experiences."

When portable video equipment was introduced some fifteen years ago, Ullman and his college friends were quick to use the new technology to produce political and educational videotapes. Says Ullman, "It was wonderful. We were in the vanguard. I tried to apply video to everything." Ullman even carved out a new major for himself, American Electronic Media, producing his thesis on videotape.

After graduation, Ullman received a grant from the National Endowment for the Arts to set up a unique television station in Monroe County, Indiana. The station operated out of the public library. Cardholders were allowed to take television courses, check out equipment, and become active in the production of programming. "It was the first such station in the world," Ullman says proudly.

The Idea

And just how does all this lead to Great Expectations? When Ullman's grant expired, he returned to California, video equipment in hand, set on producing television documentaries. "Then I heard the producer David Wolper say that if you want to eat you shouldn't become a television documentarian. It was discouraging," says Ullman.

Ullman and his wife (they were later divorced and he married someone he met through Great Expectations) wanted to eat, so he took a variety of jobs, including selling lubricant for Teflon pots and pans. For someone with his own great expectations, Ullman was not on track. But his fortunes turned around in 1975, when he heard guests at his parents' dinner party complaining about their inability to find suitable companions. "I filed it in my head," he remembers. The next day he recalled that a friend had once asked out a woman he had seen in one of Ullman's college videotapes. "That's when it snapped, and I created the idea of video dating," says Ullman. (At approximately the same time that Ullman started Great Expectations, someone in New York City started a similar service; it failed almost immediately.) Ullman rushed home to tell his wife. "She thought I was nuts," he says, "but my next-door neighbor, the actor John Savage, loved it. He told me all these stories about the lonely beautiful people in Hollywood." Convinced of the idea's viability, but without the resources to finance it, Ullman immediately sought funding from his parents. They told him to come back when he had a solid business plan.

A Market Survey and Financing

If Ullman's idea was unconventional, so was his market research. For the next several weeks, he spent all of his spare time attending singles' events. Says Ullman: "Dances, parties, seminars, workshops. I must have hit fifty or seventy-five of them. I'd either take my ring off or wear gloves. My first wife didn't like it too much."

Ullman talked to the singles he met about the dating scene. Among the topics of conversation was the question of whether or not video dating would work. "I was careful to keep the idea a secret. I'd bury it among a variety of different proposals like wine-and-cheese parties and coffee bars," says Ullman. The response to video dating was positive. People seemed to like the idea of seeing a prospective mate in an atmosphere of confidentiality. Ullman concluded that he should charge clients a membership fee for joining the service. With membership would come the right to see and be seen, and, most important, the power to select potential dates.

Armed with the results of his survey, a budget, and plan, Ullman went back to his parents, who loaned him $7,500 and cosigned for an additional $1,500 loan from the bank. His father, a doctor, also contributed the name.

Selecting a Location; Starting Up

Ullman conceived the idea in the fall of 1975 and opened for business on Leap Year Day, February 29, 1976. He had tried to obtain a patent during this period, but had given up when he realized it was the *idea* for the service — not a product, design, or process — that was novel. Although he later incorporated after the business grew, Ullman started his business as a sole proprietorship.

Aware that his audience would consist of middle-class and upper-middle-class singles, Ullman was concerned about appearances. He therefore took space in a beautiful-looking building with a prestigious address. So much for outward appearances. Inside was a bare-bones operation. Great Expectations shared a suite, a copier, and a conference room with several other small businesses. "The office I actually worked in was a hole in the wall, maybe eight feet by eight feet," says Ullman. "I had a desk, two phones, and my video equipment. It was ludicrous." But it worked. Ullman announced his opening with a strategically placed advertisement in the *Los Angeles Times* Sunday Calendar section, and the response was immediate.

Selling Himself; Promoting the Business

Ullman had been confident from the beginning that if he could get the curious in the door, he could sell them on the service, or, more accurately, on himself. "I'm a whiz with people," he says matter-of-factly. Just as Julie Brumlik banked on prospective clients' responding personally to her, so, too, did Ullman. And just as Brumlik aggressively promoted the business, so did Ullman. "I'm an old hand with public relations," Ullman says, recalling his days on the political front. Within two months, Great Expectations had been featured in *Newsweek,* the *Los Angeles Times,* and the *San Francisco Chronicle.*

Ullman was not merely Great Expectations's publicist. For the first several weeks, he was the entire staff. He met the clients at the door, escorted them to his office, then interviewed them while a hidden camera rolled. He was doing his own advertising, too. His only help came from family friends, who provided limited legal and accounting services. He had informal cash flow sheets and budget projections, but "I was winging it," he says, then laughs, "There are two reasons most entrepreneurs fail: undercapitalization and mismanagement. That was me." So why didn't he fail? Says Ullman: "My own energies, good fortune, good marketing, good idea, chutzpah, and timing. My own brilliance and luck."

Growth

By the end of its first month, Great Expectations was running at a slight profit. Still, Ullman says, "We only survived those first months because my wife was working and I was a maniac, doing the work of three persons. Seventy-five hundred dollars is absurdly low to start such a business." Much of that initial capital was spent on advertising. "This is an advertising-intensive business," says Ullman. Many service businesses are. A product or a store or restaurant has the potential to attract people just because it is seen. A service, however, is less visible. The consumer must be alerted to its existence in other ways.

The advertising worked. Ullman soon had too many clients for the small office and staff (himself) to handle. After six weeks, his mother came to help in the office. After eight weeks, Great Expectations moved to more spacious and, says Ullman, "more romantic" quarters in affluent Westwood. By this time, Ullman's father was helping, too. He would come on the weekends — Great Expectations was open seven days a week — and take out the garbage and do other chores. "We were literally a ma and pa and son operation," says Ullman.

Great Expectations attracted 500 members its first year, grossing $75,000 and running at a slight profit. The company has earned a profit every year of its existence, and now grosses close to $2 million a year. About 200 new members join each month, and at any one time there are approximately 15,000 in the membership pool. The business has expanded to several other cities. Ma and pa and son are now backed by a staff which includes skilled advertising and marketing people.

The Vision

While the scope of Great Expectations has changed dramatically, Jeffrey Ullman's vision has not. "What I created was so correct, it has held up," Ullman says. From the beginning, Ullman knew what he wanted to create on tape. "It had to be customized to the individual's lifestyle and interest," he says. "No two tapes are the same. We'd talk about lifestyles, attitudes, interests, hobbies, what they want to be when they grow up. So the ultimate result is that it is their own judgment, representative of them."

Just as the Great Expectations philosophy allowed clients, in effect, to represent themselves, it also allowed them to select their own dates. "Matchmaking is anathema to the process of self-choice and responsibility," Ullman says seriously. "I don't want to play God. If the client is successful, he should have himself to congratulate. If he's unsuccessful, he should have himself to blame. I'm a child of the sixties. I believe when you give people information, you give them power, control over their lives. We're saying to our clients, 'Now that you know about people, here's a way to find them.'"

Postscript

Although Ullman has been approached by several parties wishing to buy Great Expectations, he has no immediate plans to sell the company. "When I started, I thought I'd make a couple of hundred thousand dollars, then go back to making documentaries," he says. "And I still may." For the time being, however, he sees a parallel between his video dating service and the documentaries he thought would change the world. Says Ullman: "I think of myself as my brother's helper, a good samaritan."

LESSONS FROM JEFFREY ULLMAN

1. Do your research. Get all the information possible, then make up your own mind whether the risk is worth the reward, and if it is, do it. Just do it.
2. There is a big exception: if you have kids or other dependents, think five times, think ten times before starting. You can't be as selfish then as you can be if you're only responsible to yourself. If I were to do it now, with a wife and two kids in diapers, I'd have to have better financing from the start. I wouldn't ask my kids to sacrifice.

Those who enter the service industry are, initially at least, selling themselves as much as their particular service. If a customer — whether it's a magazine in search of typesetting or a person in search of a date — likes, respects, and trusts the entrepreneur, the new venture founded on a great idea has a good chance of surviving. But once survival is assured, the innovator cannot rest. Services, perhaps more than products or retail establishments, need to be promoted. After fifteen years in business, Julie Brumlik is still sending clever mailings to her ever-growing list of clients and potential clients, and after ten years, Jeffrey Ullman is still advertising and approaching the press with stories promoting Great Expectations. Says Brumlik: "You have to keep up incredible momentum."

4

Cashing In on the Times: Creating and Selling a Novelty or Fad Item

Our clients would ask, "What's up?" And we'd answer
that we were the Official Representative of Halley's
Comet. They'd laugh. But then at the end of the
meeting, they'd ask us to send them information.
That's when we thought: this would be fun to do.

— OWEN RYAN

The creator of the fad or novelty item, or the item centered on an event, must make hay while the sun shines, or at least while the comet approaches. It may not take seventy-six years before a chance to capitalize presents itself once more, but then again . . . The last time an entrepreneur was able to hawk T-shirts reading "Chicago White Sox: Major League Champions" was 1917.

Few of the innovators presented in this book enjoyed overnight success. It took most of them years to establish product recognition, distribution networks, good will, and good reputations. But as the case of Marvin Rosenblum and the Spiro Agnew wristwatch will illustrate, with novelties, time is of the essence. The passing fancy must be available to people in large quantities before they fancy something else.

A number of problems confront the entrepreneur wishing to market such items. First, he or she may not have the distribution network to show and sell the product to enough retailers quickly enough. In this event, the knock-off artists, many of whom do have such networks, will be quick to jump in and grab a large share of the market with their copycat items. Second, no matter how clever the item and how speedy the distribution system, stores may choose not to buy. Why? Because the novelty innovator, in all likelihood, has only one product to offer and will be out of business after the fad has passed or the novelty has worn off. Many retailers are wary because they don't know if the entrepreneur will be able to provide the quantity desired in the format desired. No matter how innovative the Pet Rock may be, it is of little value if it is not packaged properly or capable of being displayed in the store. Why, asks the retailer, should I take a chance, particularly when this probably isn't a company that I'll be dealing with again? Finally, even if the store does decide to sell the novelty, it may choose not to promote it. The best display space in the establishment may be reserved for the long-running manufacturers with more than one product line.

Discouraging as all this sounds, there are ways to overcome the barriers facing entry into the novelty field. The budding entrepreneur need not be stuck between a Pet Rock and a hard marketplace. One possible solution is to sell the idea to an existing business. A second possibility is to market more than one product, to create, in effect, an industry, so that the retail establishment must take notice.

With novelties, frivolity is the mother of invention. Need, then, will not lead anyone to the novelty maker's door. But the entrepreneur may be able to create a climate in which the consumer and retailer *demand* the product. Promotion plays an important role in generating such demand. The innovator who can attract attention to a novelty may have the comet, if not the world, by the tail. For, as Marvin Rosenblum explains, "There's a bandwagon effect. Once something is popular, everyone wants it. It's like Woodstock. Everyone wants to say, 'I was there.'"

MARVIN ROSENBLUM
– THE SPIRO AGNEW WRISTWATCH –

A Man of Ideas

Marvin Rosenblum sits down at his desk and picks up his little black book. He leafs through the pages silently for several minutes, sometimes smiling, sometimes shaking his head with a look that falls somewhere between amusement and amazement. Eventually a look of longing takes hold. "This brings back memories," he finally says. "It's been a while since I've opened this. It's got me excited again."

If Marvin Rosenblum is excited again, then Mrs. Rosenblum had best watch out. No, the black book isn't filled with names of former lovers or current mistresses, but it contains material which is equally capable of seducing its keeper. "The kind of stuff," admits Rosenblum, "that makes me jump out of the bed in the middle of the night."

Just what is it that can transform this calm, bespectacled Chicago lawyer into a man possessed? Ideas. "I'm an idea person," Rosenblum explains. "I've been coming up with ideas for as long as I can remember, writing them down in my little black book."

Rosenblum, now in his early forties, remembers his first idea as some men remember their first girlfriend. "I was twelve or thirteen," he recalls. "I thought it would be neat if you could put a patch on your arm at the beginning of the summer, which when removed weeks later would leave a word or an image because all the skin around it had been tanned. The tan-too." Rosenblum never followed through on this idea, but claims someone else eventually did. "I learned a lesson," he says. "Ideas aren't necessarily unique. At any one time there may be fifty people talking about the same idea; it's the one who stops talking and starts doing who succeeds."

Since that summer of the tan-too, some thirty years ago, Rosenblum has been filling his black book with ideas. Some have never been executed. Many have been brought to fruition. Rosenblum was the man who, in 1984, produced the highly praised movie *1984*. It was his idea to remake the film version of George Orwell's classic, and it was he who persuaded Orwell's reluctant widow to sell him the rights. He was also the creator of the ill-fated, though well-intentioned, *Hands Across America* — the effort to have several million Americans form a human chain from sea to shining sea in celebration of the Bicentennial. Less ambitious than either of these projects, but equally timely, was the Spiro Agnew wristwatch.

The Idea and the Prototype

Rosenblum feels that all of his projects try to capture or anticipate a kind of collective national mood. "I think I'm good at understanding that mood," he says. In the late 1960s, the national mood was really the national moods. The war in Vietnam had split the nation. Many officials in the administration of President Richard Nixon seemed to take the position that those who were against the war were against America. Leading the attack was Vice-President Spiro Agnew, whose alliterative campaign against the media and the liberal opposition managed to be cruel, colorful, and comical. "Nattering nabobs of negativism" is how he described the detractors. If nothing else, Agnew captured the imagination of the American public. He was a folk hero to some, the butt of a joke to others.

Rosenblum was in his second year of law school at the University of Chicago when he heard a joke that Mickey Mouse had been seen wearing a Spiro Agnew watch. "I guess law school taught me the ability to extrapolate from the abstract to the specific," Rosenblum says. Translation: he started playing around with the joke and came up with the idea and design for the actual watch.

The process was somewhat amorphous. Rosenblum is a punster. One summer he worked in an advertising agency on the Philadelphia Cream Cheese account and came up with the idea of showing a bagel and cream cheese with the slogan "On the *hole,* I'd rather have Philadelphia Cream Cheese." Says Rosenblum, "When I hear a sequence of words, I turn it over in my mind." Since Agnew was frequently accused of putting his foot in his mouth, Rosenblum determined that the watch should have feet, not hands, and that as the feet circled the dial, they should somehow end up in the vice-president's mouth.

The idea now well established in his mind, Rosenblum had to get it on paper. Recognizing that he was neither a designer nor an artist, he sought out someone to give the idea form. He had just begun to date the woman who is now his wife. She is an accomplished painter, but as Rosenblum explains, "I felt silly asking a serious artist to do this." Instead, he approached a fellow law student who had a background in art, and together they designed a prototype.

A Plan for Marketing and Production

Rosenblum did not conduct a formal marketing survey to persuade himself of the viability of the enterprise. He knew the watch could be a popular item and that the audience for the item was the growing portion of the population that found Agnew humorous, if not offensive. His intuition also told him that as the watch was going to be a novelty item, coveted for its cleverness rather than its time-telling ability, it should be priced relatively inexpensively. This sketchy information might not have been sufficient if Rosenblum were intending to go into the watch business or the novelty business on a full-time basis. But he wasn't.

The design, of course, was going to go on a watch. The next step, therefore, was to find the right watch for the project. There were two requirements for such a watch. First, it had to be adaptable; the design had to work on it. Second, Rosenblum had to be able to purchase it at a rate that would ensure him a profit when he resold it as the finished product with the design.

Through knowledgeable friends — a prime reference source for entrepreneurs — Rosenblum was able to determine that an inexpensive single jewel watch would be sufficient. The friends also directed him to several New York watch manufacturers who might serve as suppliers. Initial conversations with these manufacturers, in which he did not have to reveal his idea, convinced him that there would be little trouble in finding the inexpensive watch he needed and then adding the Agnew design.

A Plan for Distribution

The watch had potential both as a mail order item that could be sold directly at retail rates and as an item that could be wholesaled to retail establishments. As he considered various manufacturer-suppliers, Rosenblum pondered how he was going to sell his novelty. "My first plan was to distribute the watch myself," Rosenblum recalls. This approach assures the innovator total control over the operation and 100 percent of the profits, but it has its drawbacks. It is time-consuming, and it requires the expenditure of capital (in this case: the purchase of the watches, the expense of advertising, and the cost of soliciting retail outlets). The drawbacks may be worth accepting if distribution can be effected smoothly. However, it soon became apparent to Rosenblum that he did not have the preexisting network to get the watch into enough stores before someone else with greater resources copied it and beat him to the distribution punch.

"With a fad item like this you have to get a jump on everyone," Rosenblum says. "There's a critical window between the time you have your product out and everyone jumps in with the knock-offs." Although the design for the watch face could be copyrighted for protection, the concept itself was not patentable. "All anyone had to do was design their own face, put it on a watch, and introduce it into the market," says Rosenblum.

If Rosenblum had been able to devote all his energy to setting up a distribution network, he might have been able to discourage some competitors. But by now the school year had ended and he was spending the summer working long hours at a high-powered New York law firm. Marriage was also on the summer agenda. Rosenblum determined that instead of trying to control the entire enterprise, he should try to establish a partnership with an existing operation.

Looking for a Partner; Revealing the Idea

Novelty companies and watch manufacturers seemed the logical partnership candidates. They could supply the resources and outlets which Rosenblum could not. Rosenblum began to approach New York–area companies. Confident about the idea, he was uncertain what might happen when he shared that idea with the companies. The possibility existed that they would steal the idea before it even reached the marketplace. They could actually harm him more than the knock-off artists, who would only be able to steal the idea after the watch was being distributed. "I have never solved the dilemma of having to reveal an idea to a corporation with whom you want to get involved," says Rosenblum. "It's easy to get paranoid and not reveal an idea. Then you're at loggerheads. You have to have a certain amount of faith."

Rosenblum's faith was enhanced by his belief that companies might be afraid to sue him because he was a lawyer (well, almost a lawyer). "I could always sue the hell out of them," he says. Still, in his initial conversations with several companies, he never completely revealed the idea.

When Rosenblum finally found a watch manufacturer with whom he was comfortable, he did reveal the idea and the design. The manufacturer was excited by the idea, but didn't like the design. "He thought it was too negative and that the more traditional retail outlets would be reluctant to sell it," says Rosenblum. There was one other stumbling block — Rosenblum and the manufacturer could not agree upon the terms of their relationship.

Time was of the essence now. As it happened, the Swiss factories which actually manufactured the single jewel watches (the New York manufacturer adapted these watches for retail distribution) were taking their annual summer break. This meant that if Rosenblum and his would-be partner (who had thousands of watches on hand) could act quickly, they could get a crucial two-week jump on the knock-off artists (who would have to wait until the factories reopened to get a supply). While Rosenblum and the New York manufacturer hurriedly tried to work out an agreement, the new Mrs. Rosenblum rushed to create a design that would both preserve the integrity of the idea and ensure its acceptability to mass merchandisers.

Selling the Idea

The artist was successful; after staying up for almost forty-eight hours, she designed a face which showed Agnew in a less libelous pose. He looked more like Uncle Sam now. The businessmen were not so successful. The manufacturer wanted more than Rosenblum thought he deserved. Finally, Rosenblum relented. "He had me over a barrel," Rosenblum admits. "He had the critical distribution network." The deal they reached was a simple one: for a flat fee, Rosenblum sold the idea and the design to the manufacturer.

From that point forward, Rosenblum had no say or stake in the operation. The manufacturer had already rushed the design to a printer, who had printed up thousands of decals. Rosenblum watched as these decals were applied and tens of thousands of new Spiro Agnew wristwatches were shoveled into boxes for shipment around the country. "Within twenty-four hours they were in the big New York department stores," Rosenblum says, still amazed some fifteen years later.

Rosenblum says he cannot remember how much he was paid for the idea. "I think it was between $5,000 and $10,000," he says. "I made out okay." And how did the manufacturer do? "He made out like a highwayman, if not a bandit."

Postscript

As Rosenblum had sensed, the watch enjoyed great, albeit ephemeral, popularity with time-tellers from coast to coast and received much positive attention from the "nattering nabobs." Knock-off artists did enter the market. By the time the novelty wore off, there were several different watches being sold. But only one original. Today the watch is a collector's item. "I've heard they sell for as much as two hundred dollars," Rosenblum says, then shakes his head. "I think I've only got one at home. I wish I'd kept more."

LESSONS FROM MARVIN ROSENBLUM

1. Sometimes a smaller percentage of something is better than 100 percent of nothing.
2. You can't build an entire business around one fad

item. It's impossible to have the sales pipeline required to distribute the item quickly enough to beat the people who want to rip you off. In that event, it may be better to sell the idea.

OWEN RYAN
– GENERAL COMET INDUSTRIES, INC. –

It should come as little surprise that the man who bills himself as the "Official Representative of Halley's Comet" is also the proprietor of an "Imagination Agency." The brochure introducing Owen Ryan and Associates asks the question: "Which kind of agency would you rather have working for you? An advertising agency? Or an *imagination agency?*"

Confident that the latter answer was the right answer, Ryan in 1980 left the conventional advertising world to set up his unconventional service. He was not yet thirty-five years old and had risen to positions of responsibility during tenures at several top-notch agencies. What had he learned? "The single most underdeveloped resource in the business world is creativity," says Ryan, who has also run a dairy farm, worked in the federal government's Office of Economic Opportunity and written poetry.

The Idea

Ryan was using his imagination to persuade the uncreative business minds who manage America's major corporations to use his new firm, when a young New York businessman named Burt Rubin approached him. Rubin, who had made a small fortune in the 1970s manufacturing cigarette rolling paper, had a new company too. He had recently formed Halley Optical Corporation to produce the Halleyscope, an affordable telescope, and he wanted Ryan's help in marketing the item prior to the late 1985 arrival of Halley's Comet.

"I didn't even know the comet was coming," confesses Ryan. Not the kind of person who allows such minor details to sidetrack him, Ryan immediately began to research the history of the comet, which was first reported in 240 B.C. by the Chinese. To his surprise, he found that the comet had created quite a sensation on its last visit to Earth in 1910. "There were rooftop parties at the Waldorf-Astoria, comet cocktails, and the newspapers were full of stories," says Ryan.

Aware of the difficulties in selling just one item to a store, Ryan's initial response was not, "Let's create another novelty item to go along with the telescope." Rather, he tried to devise a scheme to include the product as an integral part of a retailer's own marketing program. "I happened to meet Stanley Marcus at a party," Ryan says. "I suggested to him that he create a "Heavens Department" at Neiman-Marcus. It could offer *Star Wars*–type toys, Carl Sagan's books, and the Halleyscope." Marcus was intrigued, but eventually decided "Heavens" could wait.

During one of their early meetings, Ryan and Rubin had jested that the comet's coming could be packaged just like the 1984 Summer Olympics, and had joked about setting up a company called General Comet Industries, the Official Representative of Halley's Comet. Further research by Ryan persuaded him that such a venture might not be a laughing matter. His review of old newspaper articles revealed the dramatic breadth of comet hysteria: novelties such as comet walking sticks, vitamins, umbrellas, postcards, and jewelry had captured the imagination of the 1910 consumer. The question was: Would the 1985 consumer, jaded by so many televised space-shots, care anything about the return of a comet?

Research

Ryan's research convinced him that the comet would be a sensation on its twenty-ninth recorded return just as it had been on its first twenty-eight visits, and that numerous comet novelties could be sold. United States Department of Commerce statistics indicated sales of telescopes and binoculars were booming. *Star Wars* and similar movies were drawing record crowds. And space museum and planetarium attendance was up dramatically. Equally important were the results of public opinion polls Ryan studied. "They showed that people thought the fun was missing from their lives," Ryan says.

The notion that a company built around the once-in-most-lifetimes coming of the comet could generate international fun and profits appealed to Ryan. "I liked the cosmic implications," he reflects, adding that no pun is intended. "*Cosmic* is a new word in the business lexicon. I don't think entrepreneurs devote such a tremendous amount of strength and stamina to ventures where the only reward is money. There have to be greater implications." Thus, one of Ryan's first thoughts was that an international celebration could be built around the return of the comet. Eventually, April 11, 1986, was designated as "Halley Day of Harmony."

Starting Up

Ryan has a standard operating procedure he almost always follows when he has a new idea. He incorporates a new company, even if he has no immediate plans for pursuing the idea. "That way, every year at tax time you're forced to look at the idea and see if it's worth going through the effort and expense of keeping it on the books," he explains. In late 1981, he and Rubin and a handful of others invested a few thousand dollars to create General Comet Industries (GCI). After trademarking the name and logo, they set about planning a marketing strategy.

A Marketing Plan

In devising this strategy, Ryan did what all entrepreneurs should do: homework. He visited with officials at the National Football League and the Los Angeles Olympics Organizing Committee to learn how they went about marketing. About one year after it had been formed, GCI's own strategy was in place. The company would develop particular promotions and products for particular markets such as the airlines, toy companies, and cereal makers. The products would then be licensed to the companies for a flat fee and a portion of gross sales, generally 10 percent.

More than seventy novelty items were developed. Some of them were conventional: games, jackets, bags, glassware, and calendars. Some were offbeat: a software program, a comet wine cooler ("Its contents aren't too different from the comet's," jokes Ryan), and stock certificates.

A Novelty Item: Case Study

The stock certificates serve to illustrate the Ryan imagination and philosophy. "I've learned that you should never just take an idea and run with it," he says. "It can always be built on." The idea for the certificate materialized when Ryan and his associates were trying to figure out how, as official representatives, they could actually *own* the comet. "At that point the idea was just a gimmick," Ryan says. Building on the idea, the GCI brain trust decided to personalize each certificate by printing the holder's name on it. "That gives everyone a good feeling," Ryan says. Next, a sweepstakes was created. The lucky holders of certain certificates would win cruises to view the comet. "Now everyone is saying, let's go, let's get the certificates," Ryan says. And finally, in a genuine spirit of cosmic brotherhood, GCI announced it would donate a significant percentage of certificate sales to For Spacious Skies, a Boston-based not-for-profit organization which teaches children about the wonders of the heavens. "That step gives the product *value*," Ryan says proudly.

The idea now fully developed, it could be shopped to possible licensees. "The more you can take to a company, the better," Ryan says. "You want them to be able to see, comprehend the idea." A brainstorming session quickly determined potential licensing candidates. Stock certificates suggested Wall Street, which suggested a distinguished national men's clothing chain whose haberdashery symbolized the Wall Street look.

How did Ryan protect his idea when approaching this company and others? He didn't. "Protection slows down development," he says. "You have to build on trust."

Secrecy; Promotion

While Ryan was willing to share his cosmic ideas with prospective licensees, he was not willing to reveal them to the cosmos at large. Staff members and clients were sworn to secrecy so that the general public and, more important, potential competitors, would remain in the dark. The secrecy was maintained for three years, until a November 1984 article in the *Wall Street Journal* let the cat out of the bag.

A long-time believer in the power of the press and the importance of public relations, Ryan had a timetable for promoting the venture. The article, however, forced him to speed up his master plan. He soon hired the New York public relations firm of Cunningham & Walsh. As expected, the story of GCI appealed to the media, and within a few months, Ryan had appeared on several major television and radio talk shows and the exploits of GCI had been chronicled in national magazines and newspapers across the country.

The media attention had several positive effects. For one, GCI now had instant recognition and credibility in the corporate community. The credibility was extremely important for two reasons. First, it made it easier to involve corporations as licensees. But, equally important, it positioned Ryan for post-comet adventures. Many novelty manufacturers hit and run. They have one good idea, capitalize on it, and return to their previous lives. Ryan has no such plans. "We're going to be in business after the comet," he says. "We always had to be sensitive to that."

The *Wall Street Journal* story, while a bit premature for Ryan's purposes, was hardly fatal. Ryan estimates that his three year jump on most competition secured for GCI about 70 percent of all comet-generated dollars. And dollars weren't the only currency. GCI established subsidiaries in several countries around the world.

Advertising

As the public relations campaign built up steam, Ryan tried to expand these foreign markets and establish personal contact with the American consumer. GCI mailed out thousands of slick catalogs offering everything from comet vitamins to comet Christmas wrapping paper. An advertising campaign was also started, among whose innovations were sponsored commercials reminiscent of the 1976 Bicentennial Minutes.

Postscript

As the comet neared Earth, GCI neared its projections for both cosmic and pecuniary success. Having invested several hundred thousand dollars and almost as many hours in the venture, Ryan and others found such news comforting. "At the beginning, I thought this would take about five percent of my time," Ryan says. "It's taken two hundred percent!" Ryan had hoped to gross some $10 million and contribute approximately 15 percent of that total to charitable causes.

On a far different, if not higher, plane, he had also hoped to entertain and even unify mankind by mobilizing the world to ponder the implications of the return of a heavenly body which is beholden to laws far beyond the control of human beings. "What is exciting is not selling trinkets," Ryan says, pointing to the Day of Harmony. "What is exciting is saying we played a part in millions of people getting along better."

LESSONS FROM
OWEN RYAN

1. Be disciplined in your marketing, particularly if you want to exist after the event is over or the novelty has worn off.
2. Be aware that an idea may not be your exclusive property. At any given time there may be several people who have the same idea. It's a question of who is going to act on it first.
3. Be patient. Money will eventually follow an idea.
4. Try and have a tight emotional support system. The support of a spouse can be very important.

Selling novelty or fad items or products centered on a particular event requires a sense of humor and a sense of timing. But no matter how humorous or timely the idea is, it is essential to have a marketing plan and a distribution network to implement that plan. In many cases, it is also crucial that a public relations campaign starts the bandwagon rolling and creates consumer demand.

5

Watching Out For Pet Rocks: Creating and Starting a Business Establishment

---

Define what you are after and stick to it. People came to us with the Pet Rock and told us we could sell a million of them. But the Pet Rock wasn't consistent with our philosophy. Keep to your stitching so the customer will never be confused.

— GORDON SEGAL

The entrepreneurs profiled in this chapter are a diverse lot operating diverse establishments. Gordon and Carole Segal are a husband-and-wife team who created a unique specialty shop. Michael Cullina and Steven Byer are childhood friends who, after graduating from college, opened an innovative restaurant. And William Hornig and Marcia Goldberger quit secure, well-paying jobs to open, respectively, a solar self-service laundry and a maternity shop.

Despite such differing backgrounds and vocations, these entrepreneurs share a common philosophy: *Do not try for short-term profit at the expense of long-range vision. Build.*

Each of these innovators has a vision, and each is trying to build something consistent with that vision. It may require forgoing the transitory riches promised (but not always delivered) by the next Pet

Rock, but such consistency appears to create both self-satisfaction and customer satisfaction.

GORDON AND CAROLE SEGAL
– CRATE & BARREL, INC. –

The Idea

Gordon and Carole Segal's successful and innovative chain of Crate & Barrel specialty stores was conceived at, of all places, the kitchen sink. "It was 1962," Gordon Segal remembers. "I was doing the dishes — they were classic Artzberg dishes we had picked up in the Caribbean or New York — and I said to Carole, 'How come nobody is importing this stuff in Chicago? I think there's a hole here. We should open a store.'"

The store would be patterned after the stores they had seen on their honeymoon in the Caribbean and on a trip to New York. "They were exciting," Segal says. "They carried esoteric cookware and other goods of finer quality, in greater variety, and at better prices than anything we'd seen in Chicago."

Carole Segal agreed immediately. Just out of college, she was as bored with her teaching job as Gordon was with his new job in real estate. In their early twenties, the Segals were convinced that their enthusiasm and skills would enable them to make the idea into a reality. Although Carole had no experience in the retail business, she had wonderful taste. And while Gordon's tastes, he says, were not sophisticated, he had some experience in retailing. As a teenager, he had worked in and managed his father's small restaurant while running his own business on the side. "I had a small candy company from the time I was fourteen," he says. "I operated and maintained sixty gumball machines in our neighborhood in Chicago. I'd go around on my bike filling them up and taking out the pennies." Segal loved being an entrepreneur. "When other kids were thinking about baseball and football, I was thinking about business," he says.

He had gone into the restaurant business after college, but six months spent learning the trade in New York convinced him that he should seek a different calling. Moving back to Chicago, he had become involved in real estate. That, too, however, was proving disappointing. "I've always been ambitious, driven," Segal says. "Not so much to make money, but to create. Real estate was not a creative outlet. It was solely moneymaking. I looked around and said, 'Is this where I want to be in thirty years?'" The answer was no!

Finding Products, Financing, and a Location

The Segals' first task was to determine whether they could get the wares they wanted. Within days of their chat at the kitchen sink, they were talking to Chicago-based European trade officials who could refer them to vendors of the well-designed but reasonably priced tableware and culinary equipment they hoped to introduce. "We wanted vendors willing to sell us closeouts, seconds, and in limited quantities," says Segal.

Having determined that they would be able to deal with the European vendors, the Segals turned to finding the money to pay for merchandise and for the store itself. They were able to come up with $11,000 of their own money and received a $7,000 loan from Segal's father. They sought an additional $10,000 or more from outside investors, but none could be found. Although they had only two-thirds of what they had hoped to raise, the Segals decided to proceed. They calculated that they could live for one year without any salary. And after that year? Segal did an informal *pro forma*, and the projections showed the company would have to do $70,000 in sales the first year to survive.

Location is, of course, a primary consideration in opening an establishment. The adaptability of the space for its intended use, the rent or purchase price of the space, the amount of foot traffic, the safety and character of the neighborhood, the surrounding stores, the demographics of the shoppers, the availability of parking — these and other factors must be weighed in choosing a site. The Segals knew Chicago well, and Gordon was familiar with local real estate. They settled on the Old Town area, just north of the Loop and the landmark Merchandise Mart. Why? "It was one of the areas we could afford with our limited resources, and things were beginning to happen there," says Segal. Among the things happening was the development nearby of the Sandburg Village apartment complex, home to thousands of affluent consumers who fit the customer profile the Segals carried in their heads.

The actual site was an old elevator factory, which had to be completely renovated. The Segals and the lone worker that they could afford did all the work. Carole Segal designed the interior. Because they could not afford expensive fixtures, she determined that they should sell directly out of the crates and barrels in which the merchandise was shipped (thus the name). She also developed a display method that is now widely imitated: items like wineglasses and bowls are massed in a clean-line, supermarket-style arrangement to convey that they are affordable and usable, rather than one-of-a-kind and precious.

Opening

The opening of Crate & Barrel was announced by tiny advertisements in the local newspapers. The Segals opened their doors on December 7, 1962, and prayed that they would get off to a fast start thanks to the Old Town Christmas traffic. At that time, the couple constituted the entire staff. They were understandably harried, remembering only at the last minute to stencil their logo on the appropriate places and forgetting altogether to have a cash register in the store. There was one other problem: "We had no idea how to price things because the invoices for much of the merchandise hadn't arrived yet." Segal laughs. "We ended up selling stuff below what it cost us. Of course, the customers were delighted."

Operation

Crate and Barrel did $8,000 worth of business in its first three weeks, and the Segals entered 1963 cautiously optimistic. January, however, was slow, and February slower still. "One February day we had only one sale — eight dollars," Segal remembers. "Now, whenever something goes bad, we joke that it can't be any worse than the day we did eight dollars."

Sales for the entire month of February totaled only $2,000. The

Segals' optimism began to wane. "And then," says Gordon Segal, "in the spring of 1963, Old Town broke out." The presence of artists, interesting shops, and the Second City troupe made the neighborhood the place to be. Foot traffic was excellent.

Under the guidance of President John F. Kennedy, the world trade scene blossomed at the same time. Trade barriers were removed and, most important for Chicago businesses, the Saint Lawrence Seaway was opened up. Crate & Barrel was a hive of activity. Goods shipped by vendors the Segals had never met traveled up the Seaway, were greeted by trucks, driven straight to the back of the store, and then unloaded onto a pile of tires. The Segals were so busy that they hadn't yet traveled to Europe to shop directly for inventory. But many of Crate & Barrel's customers had been abroad, and, like the Segals, had developed an appreciation for fine goods. "They saw demitasse over there and realized they could have it here," says Segal.

Carole Segal's store design reinforced the notion that the merchandise was indeed accessible. "Atmosphere, lighting, display," catalogs Gordon, "the mood is very important. This is theater." In the early days, the Segals visited other stores to observe what made for a successful atmosphere. Acknowledged masters of this art, they still make these visits. "There is always something to learn," says Segal.

Crate & Barrel exceeded its break-even mark and did $90,000 worth of business in its first year. During the store's second year, the Segals finally journeyed to Europe. "We covered it from top to bottom," Segal recalls, rattling off an itinerary that includes almost every country. "We knew exactly what we wanted," he continues. They wanted merchandise, they wanted agents, and they wanted vendors. "We built a real rapport with vendors and developed relationships with suppliers. That's important, because personality and loyalty play a much more important role with the Europeans."

Expansion

Crate & Barrel's sales were $190,000 in its second year, $290,000 the third year, and, despite losing its lease and having to build a new store down the block, $350,000 in 1965. When riots broke out in Chicago in 1967, the Segals determined that it was time to build a second store, this one in the suburbs. It was built and then followed by more stores in the city and other suburbs, and stores in Boston and Dallas. Northern California and Minneapolis are the latest venues selected.

Crate & Barrel now has 600 full-time employees and boasts a state-of-the-art 136,000-square-foot warehouse and office complex. Store and catalog sales for 1985 exceeded $50 million. In addition, Carole Segal, who retired in 1965 to raise a family, recently opened a gourmet food emporium called Foodstuffs. Its success has been so dramatic that it, too, may expand.

The Philosophy

Although he did not envision such expansion when he started, Gordon Segal is not surprised by his success. "I'm not cocky, but I don't believe there is anything I can't make happen," he says. "You have to feel that way, be driven, be a little neurotic, if you're going to succeed in any profession."

While Segal admits that profit is one of the forces that drives him, he insists it is not dominant. He could have stayed in real estate if making money were his only goal. Remembering the initial conversation at the kitchen sink in 1962, Segal says, "Our principal goal was to create something." The first piece of advice Segal offers budding retailers is this: "Don't go into business just for the money. There's so much more you have to get out of it. You have to have a philosophy, a thought process, a mission. You have to be excited, and after a while it's hard to get excited if your only goal is money."

The decision to forgo the Pet Rock is in keeping with this philosophy. "You get in trouble if you're just trying to maximize short-term profit," Segal warns. "People don't always realize it, but we don't mark things up as much as a lot of other places. Our margins are not that high. If we pay seven dollars for something, we might be able to get twenty-five for it. Instead we sell it for fourteen, sell more of it, and generate higher turnover."

To this end, while many stores try to keep expenses down and maximize profits by keeping inventories low, Crate & Barrel has always maintained high inventories. "It's our feeling that if customers see something, they want it now. They don't want to wait," Segal says. Maintaining inventory is not inexpensive. "We're constantly borrowing — very leveraged — and that can be scary," he admits.

The ability to look at the long term is what seems to separate the successful retailer from the unsuccessful one. "We don't think short-term on anything we do — signing leases, hiring employees, dealing with vendors, or dealing with customers," Segal says. Segal's obser-vations on these various elements of retailing are instructive:

On leases: "We strongly believe in investing in the physical plant."

On suppliers: "We deal with them as if we're going to live with them for twenty years."

On employees: "We promote from within. We tell people we want to build with them, that they'll have job security with us. And we give our employees a great deal of responsibility. In effect, each de-partment head is running his or her own store."

On customers: "Our goal is to make the customer happy. If the customer wants to bring something back, fine — even if the color isn't right. Whatever. If you keep the customer happy, the customer keeps coming back. We like to think of ourselves as the customer's buying agent. Our customers know what to expect."

LESSONS FROM
GORDON SEGAL

1. Don't go into business for the money.
2. Have a close associate or family member when get-ting started. Team it.
3. Be consistent.
4. Think long-term.

MICHAEL CULLINA AND STEVEN BYER
– SALADALLEY RESTAURANTS –

Gordon Segal says, "If the restaurant business had been as creative twenty-five years ago as it is today, I might have ended up doing that

71

instead of Crate & Barrel." In recent years, one of the major innovations in the restaurant business has been the salad bar. Originally designed to cater to those looking for alternatives to fast-food burgers, the salad bar has become so popular that it has actually been coopted by the burger franchises. Opening its doors in Philadelphia in 1978, Saladalley was among the first of the salad bars. Despite the competition from the McDonalds and Wendys of the world, the restaurant has flourished. Indeed, there are now several Saladalleys in the Philadelphia area collectively grossing over $3.5 million a year. The chain is moving to other cities, and its founders, Michael Cullina and Steven Byer, have plans to franchise it nationwide. Significantly, franchising has always been the plan. From the inception, Cullina and Byer have thought big and, à la Gordon Segal, thought long-term.

The Idea

Saladalley is the brainchild of Michael Cullina. As a junior at Harvard in 1976, Cullina had observed the success of one of the first salad bars in Boston, The Stock Pot. "I knew nothing of the restaurant business," Cullina admits. "But it struck me that people were attracted to the place, particularly young people, and that there were some attractive economies involved. There seemed to be a low cost of food — mostly salad fixings — and of labor — the restaurant was self-serve." This sounds like an economics or business major talking, but, in fact, Cullina was a philosophy and history major whose only previous foray into the world of business had been a paper route in his native West Hartford, Connecticut.

Convinced that the salad bar business had all the ingredients to make him a wealthy young man, Cullina called Byer, a childhood friend, and shared his vision of not just one restaurant, but a chain, beginning on the eastern seaboard and eventually extending across the nation. Byer, who, like Cullina, had no post-college plans, was a quick convert. By the end of their junior year, the two had agreed to go into business after graduation.

Research and the Plan

By the time they received their diplomas the following spring, Cullina and Byer had each worked as waiters at The Stock Pot, trying to learn as much about the business as possible. They had initially considered trying to secure a Stock Pot franchise, but their experience indicated that the restaurant was not as well run as it could be. They determined that it was best to start fresh. The original plan had been to start in Boston. But by the summer of 1977, several more salad bars had opened to take advantage of the city's sizable student population. The pair, therefore, decided it would be best to start in another city with less competition.

Finding Financing and a Location

Based on their experience at The Stock Pot, Cullina and Byer had determined they needed $40,000 to launch their first restaurant. Each was able to persuade his parents to loan $20,000 to the venture. So, armed with an impressive bankroll, the two set out to find a location.

New York City seemed a logical place to start. Figuring that the students at Columbia University had tastes similar to those of Harvard students, Cullina and Byer explored the Upper West Side area surrounding the school. They soon found what appeared to be an ideal location and began negotiations with the owner of the restaurant already on the site. They were not aided by lawyers or accountants in these negotiations. Explains Cullina, "We were skeptical of experts then. We're more respectful now. But the fees you pay can kill you. Besides, we didn't have the background to use them right anyway."

Cullina remembers the negotiations fondly. "It was one big comic opera," he says. "The owner was a Mafia-type guy who looked like Jimmy Breslin. One of his selling points was that he had rigged it so he could get electricity from next door without having to pay." The meetings with this character and the unpleasant experience of being stuck in the subway the night of the infamous New York City blackout of 1977 persuaded Cullina and Byer that the Big Apple might not be the place for their little salad bar. They scheduled a tour of Washington, D.C.

On the way to the capital, the partners stopped in Philadelphia to visit friends. There they found an ideal spot in a converted warehouse near the University of Pennsylvania. The warehouse belonged to the proprietor of Urban Outfitters, a clothing store which in more political times had been called The People's Free Store. Urban Outfitters was looking for shops and restaurants to join it in the warehouse. There was only one drawback: the space was not going to be ready for six months. Cullina, who confesses that his primary motivation was and still is "greed," was impatient. "We thought, 'We'll be old men in six months. Let's start one in Hartford and then come back and open up another one here,'" he recalls.

Cullina and Byer returned to their home town and found a desirable location — across from the Hartford Civic Center, site of concerts, athletic events, and other functions. Again they negotiated without lawyers. "We were confident and cocky," Cullina says. An agreement was reached. They could have the space for $38,000. The original Saladalley would have been in this space, but less than one week before the agreement was to be signed, the roof of the Civic Center collapsed, putting the building out of commission for months. "We raced down there, took one look, and said, 'Let's forget about this and go back to Philadelphia,'" says Cullina.

Starting Up

Go back they did, and things finally began to happen. In March of 1978, they incorporated as a Subchapter S corporation so they could take initial losses on their personal tax returns. In May they signed a lease for space in the warehouse. And in July they secured an SBA-guaranteed loan for $125,000. "We did our own plan and presentation," says Cullina. "The fact that we already had forty thousand dollars in equity from our parents was very helpful in convincing the bank." During this time, they settled upon the name for the restaurant, choosing "Saladalley" because it was located on an alley. The logo for the establishment was eventually created by a graphic artist at the university's student newspaper. Total charge: $40.

Cullina and Byer started turning their empty space into a restaurant shortly after signing the lease. They were still without expert help. No consultants or architects assisted in the design. "We used the layout of The Stock Pot as our model," Cullina says. A contractor was hired to do the major work, and Cullina and Byer did some of the minor work themselves. The results were sometimes disastrous. Once, they were so impatient to do some tile work that they worked through the night in the dark. The next morning they discovered that they had ruined much of the tile by spreading grout all over it.

While working on the physical construction of the restaurant, they also began to buy equipment for the kitchen and the dining area. This proved surprisingly easy. "Local people in the restaurant industry directed us to equipment suppliers," says Cullina. A chef was also found by word of mouth. Cullina and Byer knew someone who knew someone who had published a cookbook. Like the layout, the menu was to be similar to that of The Stock Pot — salads and soup. Says Cullina, "Our operating principle was imitation. Our *modus operandi* was comic."

Saladalley opened in December of 1978 with absolutely no fanfare. Cullina and Byer had not placed any advertisements or done any promotion. There were no banners over the alley, no signs on lampposts. Explains Cullina, "We were in a campus area where everyone knows what's going on."

Cullina and Byer were managing the operation themselves. They did $200 worth of business the first day, $350 the next, and $400 the next, all below their break-even point. The next day they ran an advertisement in the student newspaper. The ad offered a dessert coupon. Says Cullina, "We did $1,000, and we've been over break-even ever since. Knock on wood." The restaurant grossed $250,000 its first year.

Operation, Philosophy, Expansion

Over the next eight months, Cullina and Byer handled virtually every chore at the restaurant — bookkeeping, advertising, marketing, and repair work. They also took turns managing on the premises. At the same time, in keeping with their long-range vision, they were already making plans for a second restaurant. Cullina now views the collapse of the Civic Center roof as a blessing in disguise. "We could never have expanded as rapidly in Hartford," he says.

After securing a second SBA-guaranteed loan for $125,000, Cullina and Byer opened a second Saladalley. They have financed their additional restaurants with additional SBA loans (they have reached the SBA limit of $550,000) and by selling stock in 1981 and again in 1984. Echoing the words of Gordon Segal, Cullina says, "We believe in leverage."

Postscript

Saladalley now employs 250 full- and part-time workers, including a head chef, food consultant, and some fifteen managers. Salaried from the start, Cullina and Byer have yet to take money beyond their salaries out of the business. They have no other outside investments. "We believe we'll get the highest return on our money by leaving it in," says Cullina.

Although they avoided experts in their early days, Cullina and Byer are now surrounded by them. They have given an equity interest in the corporation to an experienced restaurant consultant, and even use lawyers and accountants and investment bankers. "We try to twist their arms for lower fees by saying we're growing," Cullina says.

Many salad bars, or for that matter many restaurants, come and go. "It's a deceptive business," says Cullina. "You can have a lot of cash, but that doesn't necessarily mean you're doing well." Why has Saladalley succeeded? Says Cullina, "Very early on we identified a pattern, imitated it, and then evolved and adapted to market conditions." Such adaptation was necessitated by the entry of the burger franchises into the market. "If we'd known when we started that the chains would get into this, we might not have," admits Cullina. "Their entry has forced us to position ourselves as an upscale alternative. We have to offer high quality. We've been forced to redefine the product." So, while salad and a specialty soup are still the centerpiece of the menu, other items have been added. Cullina also sees a positive side to the competition. "It has enhanced the credibility of salad bars," he says.

Such credibility can only help Cullina and Byer in their long-term quest. Wendys, McDonalds, and Burger King, beware! Saladalley is now developing a franchise prototype. Says Cullina, "We've never looked at ourselves as a small business. We always thought we'd build a chain. We had dreams of glory from the beginning."

LESSONS FROM MICHAEL CULLINA

1. Before starting, talk to people in the same field. Business people are generally willing to give guidance, and it's free. Talk to successful people. Focus your questions, so that as you go on to your next interview you can draw on what you learned from the previous one.
2. Get a background in the industry in which you plan to become an entrepreneur.
3. Evaluate the question of scale at the beginning. The bigger the scale, the bigger the return on your initial investment of capital and time.
4. Before you start, ask yourself, "Where do I want to be ten years from now?" You should also have a two-year and five-year goal. One reason we did well was that we had a long-range goal.

WILLIAM HORNIG
– SOLAR WASH, INC. –

When Michael Cullina and Steven Byer were looking for a restaurant site, one potential seller stressed that his was the ideal location because the electricity would always be free. The man was stealing it from the store next door. Tempted as they were by the prospect of free energy, the nascent entrepreneurs were set on doing things legally, and they moved on. Not far down the road from Saladalley, in Stowe, Pennsylvania, William Hornig has found a way to get energy for free, legally. Hornig is the creator and chief operator of Solar Wash, Inc., a self-serve laundry, dry-cleaning and linen service that is powered by that oldest and cheapest of sources, the sun.

When Hornig says he's watching his overhead, he means it. The laundry's flat roof houses twelve solar collectors, installed at an angle that allows them to capture the most sunlight year-round. The temperature of city water when it enters the laundry is 55 degrees. Depending on the strength of the sun, the collectors heat that water to 90 to 115 degrees. A conventional gas water heater then boosts the water temperature a few more degrees. Well-insulated storage tanks allow for slow-heating days, and an automatic pump controls the temperature if there is too great a difference between the solar collectors and the water in the tank. Although Hornig acknowledges that Pennsylvania may not be the best place to locate a solar-powered operation, he notes that his fuel bills have been reduced by approximately 33 percent.

Although the system was expensive when installed in November 1981, it should pay for itself within four to six years of installation, and it should last for thirty years. Hornig plans to be in business in thirty years, too. Like the Segals and Messrs. Cullina and Byer, he is a long-range planner with a vision. His story reinforces the notion that the most successful retailers are willing to sacrifice in the present to ensure future growth and stability.

The Idea

Hornig came up with the idea for Solar Wash after reading an article in the *Wall Street Journal* that indicated that the Laundromat industry had great potential. He had already installed solar panels atop his home, calculating that the system would pay for itself in less than four years. "It struck me that a Laundromat and solar energy really blended well," he recalls. At the time, he was a manager in a large corporation. The pay was good — he was earning $40,000 a year — but he was growing more and more disenchanted with the atmosphere at work. "As the company kept growing, it lost sight of people," he says. "It got to the point that I became a number instead of a person. I finally decided that I was better than that and that I wanted to do something that was more indicative of me."

Research

Hornig, a meticulous researcher, had spent long hours calculating the benefits of solar energy for his home. He now spent even more time researching the financial benefits of a solar Laundromat. Wisely, he did this while he was still in the employ of the large corporation. Washington, D.C., was a part of his territory, and whenever he had free time, he visited various government agencies and assembled pages and pages of information.

"I realized there was money to be made," he says. "Most Laundromats are unattended. My philosophy has always been to sell the best item at a high price. I concluded that someone should always be at the Laundromat for the customers, that there should be a drop-off business where we'd do the laundry for the customer, a dry-cleaning service, and a linen service. That way in case one service was down, the others would be working." The use of solar energy was not intended to draw customers, but rather to make the operation cost-effective. Hornig's research convinced him that this would be the case.

The idea now proven practical, Hornig did more research to figure if he could afford to leave his well-paying job. Hornig decided that the venture was financially feasible only after his family agreed to adopt a no-frills existence. "We minimized all our costs in the home," says Hornig. "Still, I wouldn't have tried it if my wife didn't have a job."

Finding Financing; the Business Structure

If Hornig was conservative on the home front, he was just the opposite on the business front. "The whole secret is leverage," he says.

"You keep your equity in the operation." Most Laundromats are in leased quarters, but Hornig determined to buy a building and to buy, rather than lease, the solar collectors. This required more money than he had.

Unlike many entrepreneurs who look for friends or outsiders to invest, Hornig wanted to go it alone. "I incorporated determined that I would be the sole shareholder," he says. "To this day, I'm president, vice-president, secretary, and treasurer. From my own experience and what I've read, partnerships don't work. If I'm going to put my neck on the line, then I'm going to call the shots. If I make it, great. If I don't, then I have nobody else to blame."

This attitude led Hornig to the banks. Before going, he put together a series of best-, middle-, and worst-case gross revenue projections. How did he make the projections? "I did extensive research on my competition, then figured the number of apartments and homes in a three-mile radius of my potential site, then figured what could be charged on a per-wash basis." After agreeing to invest his own money in the project and to put up a great deal of collateral, Hornig was able to secure a bank loan. Between his own resources and the loan, approximately $100,000 went into starting the business.

Finding a Location; Designing the Establishment

Much of the $100,000 was allocated for the purchase of a site for the Laundromat. How did Hornig find this site? He didn't. Maytag, the corporation whose equipment Hornig had decided to use, will find locations for those in Hornig's position. "Their man kept coming to me with places, and I said, 'No, no,' until they finally found the right spot," Hornig says.

Most Laundromats are spartan affairs consisting of washers and dryers and chairs lined up against the walls. Convinced that the interior of the laundry was of extreme importance, Hornig developed a different layout and then hired a local interior design firm. The result was a roomy, well-lit lounge with hanging plants, vending machines, and video games. His decision to invest heavily in the interior was similar to the Segals' method: attention to the needs of the customer, even if it diminishes short-term profits, pays off in the future.

Opening; Promotion

The opening of Solar Wash was trumpeted by newspaper ads and radio spots. "But," says Hornig, "in this business even the Yellow Pages don't work. It's all word of mouth. People know we're clean, that someone is here all the time. Some customers live as many as twenty miles away. They know if they have a problem they can come to us." Again, Hornig could save money in the short term if there were not always an employee on the premises. But, he believes, service is what brings customers back to Solar Wash.

For the first nine months, Hornig was not only the sole shareholder of the company, but the sole employee, working sixteen hours a day with no time off. As business picked up and he added the dry-cleaning and linen services, he hired help. Where did he find assistance? He watched his customers, then approached those who he thought would make reliable workers.

The Philosophy

Solar Wash's gross income has increased 50 to 75 percent each year, and now exceeds $200,000 annually. All of the money is pumped back into the business. This is possible because of the Hornig family's ability to reduce expenses and live off Mrs. Hornig's salary. William Hornig has never drawn a dime's salary. "I take money out to have lunch, and that's it," he says. "Without reinvestment you're nowhere."

Maximizing short-term profit does not interest Hornig. He is thinking long-term. "I want to add additional stores, maybe franchise this," he says. "But I don't ever want to lose track of the customers and do a slipshod job." He pauses, then with the sunny optimism typical of so many entrepreneurs, he adds: "I don't want to get over $10 million a year in sales. That's the maximum. I think after that I'd lose track of things."

LESSONS FROM
WILLIAM HORNIG

1. Do your research.
2. Don't think you can get out of there in eight hours.
3. Consider leveraging. Use the bank's money to grow instead of your own.
4. Have a bank that will go with you. Have your information defined well enough so they understand it and are willing to go with you.

MARCIA GOLDBERGER
– RECREATIONS, INC. –

Marcia Goldberger left her job with a large department store chain in 1969 to start her own business because, as she puts it, "At that time, there were no real opportunities for women beyond a certain level. I'd never been an entrepreneur before, but when you get to the point where you think your ideas are better than those of the person in front of you, then it's plain you don't like having anyone in front of you."

The Idea

A graduate of Macy's executive training program, Goldberger had moved from New York City to Columbus, Ohio, when her husband had been transferred. She had risen to divisional merchandise manager with Federated Stores when she decided she wanted to be her own boss. Having reached that conclusion rather easily, her next task was to decide: boss of what? Recalls Goldberger, "I asked myself, 'What area can I do well in and lead the lifestyle I want to lead?' The answer was maternity."

It was 1969, and recognition of the working woman was a far cry from what it is today. Recognition of the *pregnant* working woman was virtually nonexistent. Maternity clothes reflected the times. Initially the lines ReCreations carried were what Goldberger calls "Better. The affluently better." But soon, sensing that a new need was arising, Goldberger carved out a specialty — maternity clothes for the working woman.

Unlike most entrepreneurs, Goldberger has few war stories to relate. Her first store went well, as did her second and third. Goldberger, the entrepreneur, always seems to be in a state of motherhood: there are now eleven ReCreations in the Midwest, with more on the way, and there is a catalog, too. "It never really occurred to me that I wouldn't succeed," Goldberger says. She attributes her success to the fact that she knew the market so well and had excellent contacts before she started.

Financing

After she decided to open up a shop selling maternity clothes, Goldberger met with an accountant to calculate the cost of starting a new business. She already knew she would not ask friends to invest in her operation. "I wanted it clean," she says. The accountant's report indicated that between Goldberger and her husband there was enough money to finance the new venture.

Goldberger was well aware that her husband's support would be necessary. There were four children. Since Goldberger would no longer be drawing her salary from the department store, the family would have to live on her husband's income. "People like to think otherwise, but usually one of the people in the marriage is wage earner number one and the other is number two. I had my husband's salary to fall back on, so I felt no financial pressure to succeed," she says.

Her husband's salary was not her only safety net. The financial plan she worked out with the accountant was sufficient to gain a line of credit from a local bank. Goldbergers experiences in securing the line of credit were not, however, pleasant, and she has never used it. "I don't like banks because the person judging you is not a good judge. I had trouble then and still have trouble because I'm a woman. The whole thing is very offensive, so I avoid it."

Starting Up: The Advantages of Being Experienced

Those with previous experience in a business field they are thinking about entering should find Goldberger's story encouraging. Her start-up costs were relatively low. Why? "The more you know the market — the more experience you have — then the less money you need, and vice versa," Goldberger explains.

Aware of the demographics of the market she was aiming for, Goldberger found space in a shopping center patronized by the affluent. She needed money for the lease and to fix up the store, but she was able to save money because her experience in the business enabled her to design the interior. Similarly, there was little anxiety or expense in finding sources for merchandise. She knew them all from her previous job.

Before opening her doors, Goldberger incorporated ReCreations (the name was provided by her husband). "I didn't want to be personally liable," she explains. Business was brisk from the beginning. "There was little competition doing maternity for the more affluent," she says. No promotions were necessary. Goldberger had arranged to be in the Yellow Pages before the store opened and did minimal print advertising in the local newspapers.

Operation and Expansion

Goldberger, like the Segals, Hornig, and Cullina and Byer, ran the entire operation alone for the first several months of its existence. Half a year passed before she hired her first employee. "I put in a lot of hours," she acknowledges. "It's a game you have to like." She soon found that despite being her own boss, she had less flexibility than when she had worked for someone else.

Unlike the other entrepreneurs profiled in this chapter, Goldberger was, and still is, wary of leveraging. "This is personal," she says, "but I don't like being in debt." To avoid borrowing, Goldberger always funds expansion out of retained earnings. "I have never started a new store until the previous one was profitable," she says. "Stores are like children — never have another one until the last one can walk."

Expansion has been more traumatic than start-up because Goldberger finds herself unable to be in all places at the same time. "Most people who do this kind of work are perfectionists. That's a problem when you expand. You expect things to be perfect, and they're not. And they really weren't perfect when you were there alone, you just thought they were," she says.

Goldberger has gradually ceded some of her responsibilities to others. ReCreations now has some forty part-time and full-time employees. Among this number is an operations manager. Says Goldberger, "I pick the location for a new store and this person does all the hiring at the site. It's very important when you expand to define the jobs with which you need help. You know you need help, but you need to define what the person is going to do. If you can't define it well, it will be hard to find the right person."

Although she needed managerial help desperately, Goldberger found it hard to give up any power. "It's hard once you're used to running things," she says. The excitement of being in charge still moves her forward. "I'm probably making more money than I would have at my old job," she says. "I couldn't go back under any circumstances. I love being my own boss."

LESSONS FROM
MARCIA GOLDBERGER

1. Don't neglect your family. In the end what really matters is the children you have raised, not the business. That's just for ego. Although the family doesn't always perceive it that way.
2. Have experience. It's important to understand how the world operates.
3. Know exactly what you want to do. Be extremely

well defined, whether on paper or in your head. If you know exactly what you want, your chances of finding it are pretty good; if they're fuzzy, your chances aren't so good.

4. Don't make a simple business more complex than it has to be.

Marcia Goldberger echoes the philosophies of all the entrepreneurs profiled in this chapter when she says, "The plan has always been to plow the money back in. I think that's important. I never think of it as mine. It's not mine. I work for the store." The successful proprietors of business establishments seem to be able to avoid the temptation to maximize short-term profits. Such temptation is, admittedly, strong. How have they been able to avoid it? Perhaps because they recognize that forgoing short-term gains may actually enhance long-term gains. Or perhaps because they have some larger vision, something that motivates them besides profit — being creative, being the boss, building an empire. Says Gordon Segal, "We asked ourselves, 'What do we want to do? If we do it right the financial thing will take care of itself.'"

6

At Home on the Range: Creating and Starting a Home-Based Business for a Product or Service

---

I remember one time, when my daughter was visiting, I
went into her room in the morning. I was wearing a
nice dress and carrying a purse. I kissed her and said,
"I'm going to work." She looked up and said, "Mom,
you're only going downstairs."

— CORALEE SMITH KERN

While it is uncertain how many Americans work at home — the estimates range from 5 to 23 million — it is certain that the number is growing. This number includes not only individual entrepreneurs, but also the employees of major companies. Blue Cross/Blue Shield, 3M Corporation, and Control Data are among the businesses that have installed computers in the homes of workers. This phenomenon is known as telecommuting, and reinforces futurist Alvin Toffler's prediction (in his book *Future Shock*) that the workplace of tomorrow will be an "electronic cottage."

The realization by the business establishment that the home can be a viable office is evidence that home-based entrepreneurs are finally being given their due. For years these individuals had to fight institutional and governmental prejudice. Their businesses were often viewed as insignificant, and rarely were they afforded the same respect as their out-of-the-home counterparts. Fallout remains from such attitudes: in many cities, zoning ordinances and other laws still work against home workers. A discussion of this follows the profiles.

The failure to respect those operating in the home has been unfortunate. As the profiles of Coralee Smith Kern and Lynn Tatar will reveal, hidden behind the front doors of apartments and houses, there has long been a talented and innovative band of entrepreneurs.

"Home businesses are accepted now," says Kern. "The press is beating a path to the door. One reporter told me that hostages and cottage industries are the two big stories of our time." The issues Kern and Tatar face are, in many cases, different from those faced in a storefront or office building. Their profiles reveal what the innovator thinking about working at home will face.

CORALEE SMITH KERN
– MAID TO ORDER, INC. –

Coralee Smith Kern remembers with amusement her early days as an entrepreneur working out of her home in Oak Park, Illinois, a Chicago suburb. "People didn't understand home businesses, so we lied about it," she says. "We took a downtown address, and when we had to conduct interviews or meet people we rented desk space by the day in a downtown office building." Vendors who did learn of her true whereabouts were reluctant to pay calls or make deliveries. Insurance agents refused to come, and, says Kern, "The printer was obscene."

The reasons for working at home vary. For some entrepreneurs, budgetary concerns require making a bedroom or living room into an office; for others, logistical considerations (children, for example) dictate working where they wake up; still others merely prefer the convenience of commuting to an adjacent room. Kern's motivation for beginning Maid to Order in her home was more serious. In the late 1960s, she contracted the debilitating disease lupus. The illness eventually made it difficult for Kern to get to her managerial job at a manpower–temporary help company, and she was advised by a doctor to apply for Social Security benefits. She was in her middle thirties, divorced, and raising two children. "The thought of going on Social Security seemed foreign to me," Kern says. "So I thought, 'How can I earn money at home?'"

Kern was not a total stranger to the idea of working at home. When her children had been younger, she had left a different office job to raise them and had successfully operated a hand-dipped candy business out of her kitchen. The thought of returning to that did not, however, enter her mind.

The Idea

"I was looking for a business where there was a need that I could fill," she says. Confident in her abilities in the labor-contracting or manpower field, she narrowed the possibilities to three — a maid service, a legal secretary service, or a nurse service — and began to research them. All seemed feasible, and when her mother suggested the clever name Maid to Order, the Blue Chip Service, Kern was sold on the cleaning business. She decided, too, that she would focus on serving what she calls "the carriage trade," the very rich who populate Chicago's lakefront highrises. Her theory: provide better service and charge more.

Research

Before starting her business, Kern conducted a great deal of research. Her methods are illuminating. First, she scouted the competition, enlisting a friend to pose as a maid to learn how the services interviewed and paid their workers. Kern also called the services to see how they sold themselves to prospective clients. Next, in an effort to determine how well the companies in the field were doing, she sent her son to the local telephone company to look at old phone books.

Why? "You can tell how long companies have stayed in business," Kern explains. Eventually, Kern even kept her son home from school and posted him outside a Lake Shore Drive high rise to observe the flow of maids.

Her conclusion after all of this research was that "most services did not last very long because smart maids started them. They knew how to clean, but they were not business people." Kern readily admits to being a mediocre cleaner of her own house, but has always had complete confidence in her business abilities — the essential element, she was certain, to make Maid to Order profitable. "I never had any doubts that it would work."

Preparation

Her research done, Kern next set about the business of starting a business. She quickly reserved the name Maid to Order with the Corporate Division of the Illinois Secretary of State (Illinois, like most states, permits individuals to reserve names, for a slight fee, for a set period of time). Kern then sent for a small business kit from the Internal Revenue Service. This kit outlined the steps necessary to set up a business and described the various structures for a business. Kern opted for the simplest, a sole proprietorship.

Kern also requested and received aid from the now defunct Talent Assistance Program, an offshoot of the SBA. At no charge, an account from Arthur Anderson & Co. was provided to help her set up her books. At the same time, she hired an answering service. Why? Her research had revealed that most maid services did not answer the telephone; Kern wanted to offer a superior alternative.

One thing Kern did not immediately secure was insurance (she operated for six months without it). She explains that it was difficult to get. "I figured, what the hell, I'm not going to let that stop me," she says. Still, as she was going to operate as a sole proprietorship, she was taking a great risk. If an employee stole something or broke something, Kern could have ended up personally liable for the loss. Kern says that maids do not create the liability problems that most people imagine, but she does not recommend that proprietors eschew insurance.

When Kern decided to go into business, she had about $4,800 in her bank account. She was prepared to risk all of this to make Maid to Order work. But the money would be watched. Kern and the accountant drafted a precise budget and stuck to it. "We got three bids for everything," she says. For many years, she has posted sheets with the costs of envelopes and other office supplies so that her employees would understand the effect of wastefulness.

Marketing

Kern knew who her audience was — the wealthy people who lived on the lakefront. The question was how to reach them and what to say to them. She devised a two-pronged attack. First, she sent a direct mailing introducing the service to those on a "fat cat" list she had been compiling from the society pages of the newspaper. The mailing also went to all those on the polling lists in the relevant blue-stocking precincts. While mailing lists may be quite expensive, these polling lists were a matter of public record and free. As Maid to Order was billed as a "blue-chip service," she included a handsome blue chip in the mailing. The chip had the name of the service and the phone number on it. Says Kern, "I am convinced that when you kick off your business, you should have something so people will remember you. We figured people wouldn't throw away the chip."

While confident that this mailing would be a success, Kern was also moving on another front. Years earlier, she had managed a building. Aware of the tremendous influence of the building manager and doorman, she approached these people at several high rises and promised them commissions for any referrals.

Hiring

With the marketing plan well established, Kern was ready to fit the final piece into the puzzle — hiring the maids. She placed an ad in local newspapers, and using the downtown office space, which could be rented by the day, began the interviewing process. Her son went into the city to conduct the interviews. Kern remained home, checking references. Again, she felt confident in her abilities. "If there's one thing I'm good at, it's evaluating talent," she says.

Kern has never had a problem finding maids. Why? She pays more than her competitors. But more important, she says, "I treat them with dignity." She strongly believes that maids, accustomed to being given little respect by their employers, care as much about the way they are treated as the amount they are paid. "Our maids know we'll look at both sides of the story if a client complains. And if they're in the right, they know we'll go to bat for them. We've dropped clients who haven't been fair to our maids," says Kern. This is not the case at most other services.

Starting Up

Kern sent out her first mailing in mid-November 1971 and sent her first maid out about one week later. Six months had elapsed from the day she had decided to go into business. Her home was now an office, too. To make the operation as professional as possible and to maintain her own discipline, Kern set aside a specific area of the house as a workplace. The front porch was appropriated, as was her son's room. He moved in with his sister.

Business was brisk from the beginning; Kern had done her home-work. Within three or four months, Maid to Order was running at a nice profit. The lakefront residents weren't the only people signing up for the service. An ad Kern had placed in an Oak Park news-weekly was also generating a good deal of business.

Kern's only difficulty was keeping the cash flow under control. She was paying her maids every week, but it took time for the clients to pay her. A minor adjustment solved this problem. Kern started pay-ing the maids every two weeks and began giving clients a discount if they left a check on the day the maid came.

Operation

As the only person running the entire business, Kern ran into prob-lems as her illness progressed. During its early years, Maid to Order flourished when Kern was healthy, but foundered a bit when she was ill. "I hadn't trained anyone else to take my place," she says. Her mother would come to help, but, says Kern lovingly, "She's a born-again Christian and her approach to the business was to say, 'Let's everyone pray for Cora.'" Eventually, Kern hired backup support.

Promoting the Business

Whenever possible, Kern continued her direct-mail effort and supplemented it with clever marketing promotions. One campaign centered on the theme that Maid to Order kept homes "fresh as a daisy." Kern ordered 100,000 daisy magnets, then gave them to maids to leave on the refrigerator doors in the homes they cleaned. At the same time, pots of fresh daisies accompanied by a large bag of magnets were delivered to building managers up and down the lakefront.

Kern did little advertising the first few years and made no effort in the public relations area. Then, with her company's annual billings well into six figures, Kern was approached by a Fortune 500 corporation that wanted to buy Maid to Order. "I figured I must have something here," Kern says, laughing. Her response was not to sell, but to promote the business so it could grow even larger. She undertook an extensive public relations campaign which continues to this day. As a result, the business has been featured in numerous newspapers and magazines across the country, and Kern has emerged as a leader of the home-business movement. She has appeared on several television shows, including the syndicated "Donahue" show and ABC's "Nightline." The wise entrepreneur is the one who does not wait to see how such publicity will affect the business, but rather *uses* the publicity to advantage immediately. Kern sends reprints of the articles to clients and prospective clients.

Kern is so convinced of the importance of publicity that she has now created her own public relations agency to promote Maid to Order. "There was a one-page article about Maid to Order in *Family Circle*," says Kern. "We figured that to take out a one-page ad in the same magazine would have cost about $37,000. Publicity is free advertising."

The Workplace

Maid to Order is no longer based in Kern's small house in Oak Park. Kern and her offices have moved to a five-bedroom town house in Chicago's fashionable Lincoln Park area. But success has not changed the Kern philosophy about working in the home. "You have to have discipline," Kern says. Even when she is ill and unable to dress for work, Kern changes into her best socks and flannels before going to her desk.

A specific part of the town house is designated the office. This is important to maintain a sense of professionalism and also for tax purposes. A tax write-off may be available based on those portions of a residence devoted exclusively to business (it is advisable to consult an accountant with respect to the tax implications of working in the home).

Postscript

Maid to Order is today a thriving and lucrative corporation (as the business got bigger, Kern changed its structure), with franchises available for purchase. The company employs hundreds of maids and several office workers. The business offers a variety of services it did not offer when it opened in 1971; the company now provides bartenders and waiters and waitresses for parties, as well as maids to clean apartments maintained by corporations. This latter effort has been particularly successful. Kern was among the first to see this market emerging and used her contacts with the "carriage trade" to gain access to corporate as well as personal apartments.

While Kern's lupus sometimes keeps her down, she manages to pursue an extremely active schedule, which includes public speaking engagements, television appearances, and appearances before legislative bodies dealing with issues related to home businesses, particularly zoning. How does she manage? "I always thought that if you worked hard and prayed, you'd succeed," she says. "When I got sick, I was afraid I couldn't meet that ethic. But I've found that the key is working *smart*. I've learned to husband my energy. I never make the same mistake twice; that's unforgivable. Work smart, not hard, and you can succeed."

LESSONS FROM
CORALEE SMITH KERN

1. Plan your work, and work your plan. Be self-disciplined: set aside time for your work and follow your business schedule. Remember that you are at work and have no time for visiting friends.
2. Prepare a definite place to work, one that is dissociated from the rest of the house.
3. Always get up, get dressed for business, and *go* to work.
4. Be a professional and hire professionals. Get expert advice on taxes and business laws, and go steady with your accountant.
5. Install a separate business phone and get an answering service.
6. Always have a backup person, someone who knows the ins and outs of your business so that it never stops functioning.
7. Keep in touch with the outside world. Join a professional association and read the financial papers. Subscribe to trade journals in your field — many of these are free.

LYNN TATAR
– THE AMAZING CHOCOLATE FACTORY, INC. –

Lynn Tatar has little in common with Coralee Smith Kern. Where Kern had business experience before starting a home-based operation, Tatar had none. Where Kern's children were older and able to help with the business, Tatar's two children were both preschoolers when the business began. And, most important, whereas Kern was forced to work because of economic necessity, Tatar had no such pressure. Her husband was, and still is, earning a comfortable living as a bank vice-president. As Tatar, who had quit a teaching job to have the first of her two children, confesses, "I wasn't even restless. I had plenty to do raising a child. I loved being at home. Going into business was the farthest thing from my mind."

How, then, did she become an entrepreneur? Like a growing number of housewives, she discovered she had a talent — in this case, creating candy novelties — which would allow her to stay at home, raise a family, and also have the satisfaction of building up a business and a bank account.

The Idea, Research, and Starting Up

The Amazing Chocolate Factory grew out of Lynn Tatar's amazing ability to make decorative chocolate delights for Tatar family functions. This was before the boom in chocolate specialities. Says Tatar, "It was kind of new then. And when people saw them, they told me I should go into business." Among those pushing the hardest were her husband and father, both of whom are business-oriented. "My father kept saying, 'I don't see how you can't make money,'" Tatar says.

Tatar dismissed the notion until 1981, when she was confined to bed during part of her second pregnancy. "What do you do when you have to sit for a month?" she says. "I started calling wholesalers to figure out how much the things for a business — chocolate and molds and packaging — would cost." She found these wholesalers in the Yellow Pages.

Tatar determined that relatively little money, perhaps $500, would be needed to start on a small scale. Still, she was hesitant. "With another baby coming, I had no idea what kind of time I'd have," she says. Her husband and father finally persuaded her. "I figured that the worst thing that could happen was that if I didn't sell enough chocolate the family would eat it," Tatar smiles. "The way I looked at it, we weren't dependent on this money. It's like you have five hundred dollars and buy a stock. It's a chance."

Now excited, Tatar began almost immediately. "We were afraid if we didn't get into it, we'd miss the boat. The chocolate craze was just beginning then," she says. Still pregnant, Tatar called several wholesalers, and ordered the best products at the most reasonable prices.

There was never any question *where* Tatar's business would be located: at the site where she had already been making chocolates, the Tatar kitchen in a suburb north of Chicago. Would that be legal? She called the city Zoning Board and found no difficulty at that level. But the county in which Tatar lives requires a license for a food establishment, and such an establishment must be, says Tatar, "a separate facility."

The Tatar kitchen did not qualify as separate. Says Tatar, "We seriously considered not doing it, but I knew there were so many people doing similar stuff who weren't licensed that we decided to go ahead." To cover potential difficulties, however, Tatar did secure liability insurance that would cover any problems she ran into without a license.

Marketing

While discovering the sources and costs of her material, Tatar had also been busy defining her market. "I made a list of outlets for the candies," she says. Upscale gift shops and food and candy stores were the retail outlets she imagined. In addition, Tatar thought corporations and country clubs and churches and synagogues could use customized candy for their own purposes, as gifts or for fundraisers. Finally, she counted on serving individual customers who would want the chocolates for birthdays or weddings.

After targeting these outlets, Tatar went to the public library and compiled a list of corporations and their officers, then sent a direct mailing explaining her new business. Direct mail, apparently made to order for Maid to Order, was a bust for The Amazing Chocolate Factory. "I quickly discovered they had to see samples to appreciate what I was offering," Tatar says.

After taking time out to have her baby, Tatar began to schedule personal calls on prospective corporate accounts. This, of course, necessitated being away from her new baby and other toddler, and away from the kitchen where she was chief cook and bottle washer for the candy orders. Realizing she could be neither a mother nor a candy maker if she was out selling, Tatar enlisted her mother to help out at home and started paying calls. "I wore the one good post-maternity dress that I had," she remembers. She carried photos of samples and some samples themselves with her — everything from chocolate golf balls to more risqué adult novelties — and a price sheet. Her prices were based on her costs and what her competition, the upscale chocolatiers, charged for similar items. Tatar admits that she was nervous about calling on the corporations, but says she quickly grew to enjoy the selling. "I'd never done anything like it before," she says. "But I found I had a good sense of business."

The Workplace

The thought of turning a house with young children into a "factory" (even if it is a chocolate factory!) no doubt deters some individuals from pursuing new ideas. Tatar's home is a comfortable but modest one. To accommodate the tools of her trade, not only the kitchen, but the garage, living room, and even bedrooms must play host to chocolates, molds, packaging, and corporate records. During the holiday gift season, which extends from October through Valentine's Day, the Tatars are almost prisoners of the business. But this incarceration doesn't seem so terrible with the smell of chocolate wafting through the house.

Many would-be home-based entrepreneurs fear that their children may wreak havoc on the business. Chocolate candies seem particularly susceptible to light-fingered juveniles. But Tatar's fears that her youngsters and their friends would become samplers of her samplers has never been realized. Says Tatar, "We have set down rules about this. The kids know Mommy has a business, and that they're not allowed to bother it. I've explained that it's lucky I can work at home, because a lot of mothers can't. The kids like that, too, so they co-operate." Still, Tatar admits she is not above bribing the preteen set with chocolates.

Until her youngest child was finally old enough to go off to nursery school, Tatar worked only during nap time or in the evenings.

She now has more time to devote to the business, but, she says, "A lot of times I'm up until two in the morning." Burning the midnight oil while heating the chocolate is required, says Tatar, "because there are always distractions at home. I'm either getting dinner cooked, or the laundry done, or running to parent-teacher meetings." But of these "distractions" Tatar says, "I'm not going to give those things up. My kids are still my number one priority."

Structure and Help

Tatar began business as a sole proprietorship because, she explains, "I wanted to make sure if we'd make it go." Once the business was doing well, she incorporated. In matters such as these, she feels fortunate that advice is no further away than across the dinner table: her husband has a law degree and has provided legal and accounting help. He has assisted with the company's bookkeeping and periodically does financial projections. Tatar has help in the kitchen, too. Her mother and a local high school girl (found through the Youth Employment Service) are, in effect, "sous-chefs." The sous-chefs are particularly busy now that Tatar has hired a manufacturer's representative to sell the chocolates across the country. Paid on a commission basis, the representative carries samples of Tatar's candies and makes calls on gift stores and other retail outlets.

Postscript

Although The Amazing Chocolate Factory is not trying to break into the Fortune 500, Tatar has built a comfortable nest egg that will pay for her children's college educations, and more. The business grosses approximately $15,000 a year. As Tatar's costs and overhead are relatively low, most of that money goes straight to the bank. Tatar recognizes that she has the luxury of not needing this money, but has resisted the temptation to spend it frivolously. "I have friends who work out of the home and consider what they earn 'mad money.' But I've never felt that way. I've always treated this as a business."

Tatar is now willing to expand the business. She admits such expansion is overdue, but says it was impossible to consider until both her children were in school. "The business hasn't taken off as quickly as it could have," Tatar says. But she is not complaining. "We're making money, and I love what I'm doing," she says. "I'm not prepared to go out of the home and work."

LESSONS FROM LYNN TATAR

1. Keep your sense of humor.
2. It can be done. I would encourage people to try. I originally thought that because I had children I couldn't do it. But there are enough hours in the day.
3. Don't overextend yourself in terms of money. Don't lay out $1,000 for something you may not need. A lot of people think you need a lot of glitter to make it go. That's not necessary. It was several years before we even spent the additional money to put in a business phone. It just wasn't necessary at first.
4. Set ground rules with your children as situations arise.
5. Have the support of your husband. If my husband were against this, we wouldn't be doing it. But he's very helpful and supportive. You need that. Otherwise there may not be time to do everything with the business and the family.

ZONING AND THE HOME BUSINESS

Years before Lynn Tatar opened The Amazing Chocolate Factory, Coralee Smith Kern made and sold hand-dipped candies in her home. Kern eventually stopped. "I had a cat, and I didn't have a health permit," she explains. "I was afraid. I thought I was being a bad girl. I was intimidated."

Kern is no longer intimidated. Because she has an electric stapler, calculator, and typewriter, Kern is in technical violation of an old

Chicago ordinance that prohibits "the use of electrical devices in home businesses." She has no intention of folding her tent. "If they think I'm running a sweatshop, they can pay my air-conditioning bills this summer," she once told a newspaper.

The absurdity of the Chicago ordinance is sometimes matched by the absurdity of those who enforce it. Not too long ago, a husband and wife, both writers, were ordered to stop working at home because they used word processors. If strictly enforced, the ordinance and others like it across the country could have a devastating effect on millions of Americans who use computers in their home-based ventures. Federal laws seem equally outdated. The "Seven Prohibitions" added to the Fair Labor Standards Act in the 1940s make it illegal to make for sale jewelry, buckles, belts, gloves, mittens, or embroidery at home. Sewing men's clothing is permitted, while sewing women's clothing is taboo.

Such archaic and restrictive regulations have led Kern and thousands of others to unite and press governmental bodies to create a climate conducive to home business. Several years ago, Kern formed the National Association for the Cottage Industry to serve as an informational clearing house for those working at home and to lobby for home-based business people. The organization does not oppose all regulations. Licensing, inspection, workers' compensation, and minimum-wage requirements have a place in the home as well as the office or factory, Kern acknowledges.

The Association, which provides an ideal opportunity for networking, is now several thousand members strong. Members receive, among other things, a semimonthly newsletter, resource guides, and the opportunity to join a group insurance plan. Seminars are also offered. For more information write:

National Association for the Cottage Industry
P.O. Box 14460
Chicago, IL 60614

If you are thinking about working in your home, you should contact the local zoning board to determine the relevant zoning ordinances. If your business is one, such as a food service, that might require licensing, permits, or inspection, contact the appropriate city, county, or state agency. Obviously, many individuals operate cottage industries that are in technical violation of any number of regulations. Until those regulations are removed, the budding business person must decide whether or not to join the crowd of scofflaws. You may want to consult a lawyer to evaluate the implications of various alternatives.

Despite some restrictive zoning regulations, operating a business out of the home has become an appealing and realistic proposition for a growing number of Americans. As the profiles of Coralee Smith Kern and Lynn Tatar demonstrate, different circumstances, needs, and desires may combine to lead innovators to choose the same workplace. Whether the venture is a full-time necessity or a part-time luxury, certain steps must be taken to create a climate for success. A simple but often forgotten principle should guide the home-based entrepreneur: be professional. Treat your business as a business.

7

Moonlighting: Creating and Starting a Part-Time Business

Some people urge me to devote myself to the business
full-time. I get a tremendous joy being involved, but
there's nothing I can do full-time. I could be there
twenty-four hours a day. What would I do? Label
cassettes? You should set it up and have the guiding
sense of where it's going and continue to nudge it. If
you design it right, it should be able to be run by
others.

— DUVALL HECHT

The idea, powerful and right, came to him on the Los Angeles freeway. Why waste the two or three hours spent commuting each day
listening to the same pop music on the car radio, the same news, the
same talk? Why not read a book? The demands of his profession and
his family had made it difficult to escape into the world of literature
he had always loved. It would be wonderful to use this dead time
spent on the road to reintroduce himself to the classics, taste modern
fiction. It was 1971 then. Duvall Hecht spent the next two years
trying to find something he could slip into his portable cassette
player. "At that point, I was just looking for something to listen to,"
Hecht remembers. "I wasn't thinking about starting a business."

How could he? Hecht, a securities broker, was already on the fast track at a well-respected investment firm, and he was teaching crew at a local university. How could he find the time to market books that were on tape?

Elaine Cogan was not thinking of starting a new venture either. She was busy enough as a full-time business consultant and writer. Then she wrote a letter to the *New York Times* complaining that tea drinkers were second-class citizens. So dramatic was the response to her letter that she, too, had to determine whether she had the time to wear yet another hat and sell fine teas through the mails.

Time is the nemesis of many innovators. Unable to quit their jobs (perhaps because they love them, perhaps because they need them), these people are faced with the unhappy prospect of seeing their great ideas turn sour because there is no time to pursue them. The profiles of Duvall Hecht and Elaine Cogan should provide inspiration and instruction to those busy individuals who worry that there are not enough hours in the day to chase a dream.

DUVALL HECHT
– BOOKS ON TAPE, INC. –

A Market "Survey"

In an effort to find recorded books, Duvall Hecht contacted everyone and every place that came to mind. "I didn't realize it, but I was researching the market," he says. He tried public libraries and publishing houses, even the Library of Congress. What did he find? The cassette having been perfected only in 1965, most recorded material existed on records, reel-to-reel tapes, or eight-track tapes. On cassettes, a fairly wide selection of "talking books" was available, but only to the blind and physically impaired; the Bible was available to the general public; and professional materials for lawyers and accountants existed. Hecht did manage to find a recording of James Mason reading A. E. Housman's poetry. But the cassette cost ten dollars and occupied only one day's commute. "To put together a library at that rate would have broken me," Hecht says, laughing.

Further research uncovered a company offering a limited number of books that were in the public domain. "But," says Hecht, "you had to pay sixty dollars for Lord Chesterfield's letters to his son. After listening to something like that, then what do you do with it?" Hecht was frustrated. He couldn't afford to get all he wanted, and there were no contemporary books available.

The Idea and the Idea Man

"There was a progression," Hecht says. "I looked at the freeway one morning. It was five A.M., and it was already jammed with people like me. And I thought, 'There are thousands of people out there who need books, too.' I thought, 'If it isn't available, I'm going to make it available.'"

The fleshing-out process was almost instantaneous. "The name Books on Tape came to me because I figured that's what I was after," says Hecht, his voice still full of excitement as he relates events that took place fifteen years ago. "Then I figured it could be a lending library, and from what wasn't there, I deduced what should be there." Hecht, who disliked abridgements, wanted full-length readings. He wanted current books, not just classics; rentals, not sales. As for distribution, "It had to be mail-order," he explains. "Because how else could I afford to distribute it?"

Hecht is an individual who devotes his utmost energy to the task at hand, whatever that may be. After competing in the 1952 Olympics in paired oars and failing to win a medal, he and his partner worked religiously and won the gold medal four years later. "The first time it was a thrill just to get there," Hecht says. "The second time we were entirely focused on winning."

Winning may be viewed as both a blessing and a curse. Says Hecht, "I remember rowing back from the reviewing stand and thinking, 'What are we ever going to do where we have such a sense of purpose again?'" It took several years to answer that question. After a stint in the military as a pilot, he drifted for the next several years — working as a pilot for Pan Am; getting a master's degree in journalism at his alma mater, Stanford; teaching, and coaching crew.

Finally his father, who headed a large securities firm, persuaded him to use his journalistic skills to write for the company's research department. Hecht soon moved on from his father's firm to another one, but he has worked in the securities field for the last two decades.

When the idea for Books on Tape struck him, he was devoting an Olympian effort to becoming the head of the securities firm at which he was then a middle manager. He had no intention of giving up that effort, which he was certain would be rewarded. "I just wanted something to read," he says. His initial plan was to find a partner ("a white knight," he says) who might take the idea for Books on Tape and make it a reality.

Finding a Partner; More Market Research

While Hecht was convinced that every commuter on the freeway was waiting for the opportunity to rent recorded books, his wife and friends were not persuaded. How, then, could he persuade a potential partner? More market research was needed. Hecht was in an ideal position to conduct the research. With the luxury of having a well-paying job and a base of operations, he could work on the new project in his spare time.

In *her* spare time, his secretary at the securities firm designed a letterhead for Books on Tape. Then Hecht composed a letter. "The letter said: here's our service — best sellers on cassettes, rental, mail order, no deposit," remembers Hecht. "It didn't ask for money. It said if you want more information, write." Hecht could hardly ask for money. "There was no company and no rights to any book at that time," he admits.

The letter was sent to 500 people in a local university alumni group. The members of the group fit Hecht's profile of his imaginary customer — the affluent commuter. Experts agree that a one to two percent response to a direct-mail offering is more than adequate. Five percent of those queried responded to Hecht.

Armed with the encouraging results of his survey, Hecht was able to interest a good friend in the project. Bill Jenkins (not his real name) was also a former colleague. In his early thirties, he had gone into semiretirement after making a small fortune in the securities business. He had initially viewed Hecht's idea with skepticism, but he was a marketing man and was impressed with the survey results.

Jenkins seemed the perfect partner. Says Hecht, "He was a terrific implementer, and he had spare time and cash. He looked like my white knight. Remember, I was still a working boy expecting to be president of my firm. I thought I'd just be helping on the literary end."

A partnership was formed with a handshake, and Jenkins and Hecht each put up $4,000. Why that sum? "That's how much I sold my old Porsche for," Hecht says with a laugh. This was typical of the somewhat haphazard fashion in which the partners initially operated. They did not talk to lawyers, accountants, or bankers. "We were still in the brainstorming stage," explains Hecht.

In addition to his work at the securities firm, Hecht was also coaching a college crew team. "Books on Tape was the third thing I wanted to do," he says. "I was just happy to turn things over to Bill. I figured fifty percent of something is better than a hundred percent of nothing."

In January 1974, Jenkins took the first big step toward bringing Hecht's idea alive. Aware that rights to books had to be secured before the books could be recorded and distributed, Jenkins hired the well-regarded Beverly Kempton to introduce him to publishers and agents. Kempton had helped to legitimize *Playboy* some years earlier by securing respected short fiction for the magazine. Soon Jenkins was in New York meeting with the two dozen or so individuals who controlled the subsidiary rights to the kind of books that interested Hecht.

"Unfortunately, that was Bill's high point," says Hecht, with no animosity. Upon his return to California, Jenkins quietly disappeared from the picture because of personal problems. He did not even send thank-yous to those he had met. He had also promised to execute a contract that would arrange for the granting of recording rights and then to send that contract to interested parties. A year went by and the contract had still not been executed. Hecht realized that the valuable Kempton contacts were being lost. "I was waiting for Bill to do something," says Hecht. "I hadn't made the mental adjustment that I was going to have to handle any of this."

When the college crew season ended in June 1975, Hecht reevaluated his position vis-à-vis Books on Tape. "I decided, 'If this thing is going to work, I'm going to have to do it now.'"

Moonlighting: Part One

How did Hecht, still pushing for the presidency at his full-time job, find the hours and energy to work part-time on Books on Tape? He did this moonlighting at sunrise.

Because he lived in Newport Beach, a substantial commute from his Los Angeles office, Hecht had kept a small apartment close to work. Now he would rise at home by 3 A.M., drive to the apartment, and then call the contacts developed in New York some eighteen months earlier. He would make four or five calls between 5 and 7 A.M. Los Angeles time, and perhaps be able to speak with two or three of the parties he sought. Then it was off to the securities firm.

Hecht had targeted the titles he wanted, but admits he was not certain how to secure the rights to put them on cassettes. His first few calls were awkward. "Looking back, it was labored and painful," he recalls. "But it's clear that at some point I felt this idea deserved to see the light of day. It proves that if the idea is strong enough, it will support minor errors."

Here, the minor errors were that Hecht did not have a handle on the vocabulary of publishing and that he had lost some credibility by failing to contact these people for a year and a half. Hecht was helped over the first hurdle by a friendly subsidiary rights editor who liked his idea. He helped himself over the second hurdle by explaining that it had taken several months for Books on Tape to find financing and to draft the best contract possible. "I was bullshitting," he says now. Some agents and publishers hung up, but some gave him rights in return for a 10 percent royalty on rentals.

Hecht attributes the success he had at this point and in the years that followed to the professional image projected by Books on Tape, notwithstanding the eighteen-month gap. "Beverly Kempton was important," says Hecht, "and the legal work, once it was done, was first-class. It wasn't like we were a couple of guys who just flew in from Toledo. The people in New York felt comfortable with us. The appearance was of a first-class operation. 'Legitimacy' is the perfect word."

Going into Production

Having secured the rights to a handful of books, Hecht's next job was to get the books onto tape. This was a complicated task. A system for actually producing the tapes had to be developed (Hecht received help from a friend who was a stereo expert). Tapes had to be purchased in quantity (Hecht found wholesalers in the area). Readers had to be found (unwilling to pay union scale to actors, Hecht placed an ad in *Variety* and was inundated with letters from talented, but starving, nonunion actors).

This preliminary work done, the tapes had to be produced and edited. Here, the busy Hecht turned matters over to his wife Sigrid. Why? In part because he was busy with his job and crew, but also, he says, "Because I trusted her. She's a meticulous seamstress, and I knew she'd be a meticulous editor."

Selling the Product

In its infancy, Books on Tape produced about four books a month. *Paper Lion* by George Plimpton was the first offering. H. L. Mencken's *Happy Days* was next. "It was exciting, like it must have been when the first Ford rolled off the assembly line," says Hecht. "Here was this tiny little factory with all the elements in place." Unfortunately, the Ford analogy must end here. Hecht's tiny factory was in his bedroom, and there existed no dealerships to sell the product to the public. It was fall 1975. Hecht was gearing up for the autumn rowing season at UCLA and the autumn selling season at the securities firm. Now he had a third season to worry about.

The cost of producing the tapes had pushed Hecht over his $8,000 budget, and he had no more Porsches to sell. "I didn't have any money. I couldn't launch an extensive advertising campaign, so I ran a one-inch ad in the *Los Angeles Times*," he says. At the same time, he sent a direct mailing reminiscent of his first survey letter. The disappointing response to this mailing surprised him. "It just proves that while people may want information about a product, they won't necessarily buy the product," Hecht says philosophically.

The newspaper advertisement did generate a small response. Orders began to trickle in. "It was exciting to see the books go out," Hecht says. "But it was even more exciting to see them come back." Books on Tape was, and still is, operated on the honor system. There is no return deposit required.

Moonlighting: Part Two

Hecht insists that his work at the securities firm was not affected by his work at Books on Tape. "I'm very compartmentalized," he explains. "To be successful in the twentieth century you have to be compartmentalized, multi-channeled. I could do the Books on Tape work at home at night, planning with Sigrid, duplicating tapes." He still rose early in the morning to call New York and get more books, and on his way from the securities firm to crew practice, he would stop at the post office to pick up or send out cassettes.

Soon he felt a growing disenchantment with his full-time job and a growing infatuation with his part-time exploits. When the idea for Books on Tape first came to him, Hecht was certain that he was on his way to becoming president of his firm. "I thought by being a hard worker that I would get taken care of," he says. Eventually, it became apparent that this was not to be. "It's common and terribly frustrating, but sometimes you overestimate yourself or there aren't enough spots and things don't work out," Hecht says. "It was killing me. I had all this energy and drive, and here I was stuck in middle management."

Hecht's position, as he indicates, was not unusual. Many happy entrepreneurs were formerly unhappy middle managers who had the confidence and desire to control their own destinies and build their own companies. There was a silver lining in Hecht's cloud. As disappointing as his situation was, it did provide him with a comfortable income; by staying at the job, he could continue to earn that income while he devoted his off hours to his new idea.

The first cassettes cost about $2,000 apiece to produce. The rental charge, including shipping, was in the neighborhood of $10. Although economies of scale later came into play, the pragmatist might argue that a lot of rentals would be required just to reach a break-even point. Hecht, the optimist, had no trouble envisioning those rentals. "It was such an obvious idea. I didn't see how it could fail. I thought the business would take off like a stripe-assed zebra."

But it didn't, and as Hecht drove to work each morning, he looked out at the other commuters and tried to fathom why they weren't all listening to Books on Tape. He remained confident. "If you don't have the capacity to believe in something, you're not going to get it done," he says. When more money was needed to keep the business going, he dug into personal savings. "I set no limits on time or money," he says. "After all, the central idea — that you could record full-length and people would rent and return — was working. Those are the elements of a helluva business!"

By the end of 1975, Hecht had contributed about $20,000 of his own money to the endeavor. He never thought about borrowing the funds. "There's less anxiety when you lose your own money than when you lose the bank's money," he explains.

Operation

In 1976, Books on Tape's first full year of operation, sales were approximately $17,000. Expenses were approximately $50,000. Advertising and other marketing efforts were stepped up (Hecht made several speeches to local groups, for example), and sales the second year jumped to $170,000. Says Hecht, "Our first two years were really research and development. We were experimenting with the design of our format and the catalog advertising our books. There was a recession going on, too. We thought that it wouldn't have an impact on us, but it did." There were other glitches: "Our pricing was too low, and our mailings weren't frequent enough. We used to think that we could watch expenses by not mailing every month, but found we were actually losing business. We're a mail-order company."

Third-year sales were $370,000. Although the company was not yet running at a profit, Hecht's faith in the idea was beginning to be rewarded. In 1979, he quit his job coaching crew to devote more time to Books on Tape. He also left the securities firm, where he was stagnating, to join another firm. Early mornings were still devoted to Books on Tape, while business hours were devoted to the new job. By this time, Sigrid Hecht was working full-time on the venture. Soon, another friend, convinced of the viability of the idea, purchased equity in the company, and the drain on Hecht's wallet was eased.

Although Books on Tape's revenues have increased every year, the company has just begun to show a profit. Sales are now approximately $3.5 million per year. The company has moved out of the Hecht home into its own building. Sigrid Hecht still manages the operation, overseeing about thirty-five employees who process mail and telephone orders. Sigrid is salaried now, but Duvall Hecht has only drawn a salary for one brief period in the company's history. In 1984, in between a job with a securities firm and work with a real-estate syndication company, Hecht devoted six months of full-time work to the company and drew $4,000 a month from the coffers.

Moonlighting: Part Three

After working full-time for Books on Tape in 1984, Hecht concluded that the rapidly growing venture still does not require his undevoted attention. "It takes more than one person to run it, but not really two," he says, noting that his wife is doing a fine job. "It's a very simple idea, and all that is required is getting it to run smoothly." Still, he would like to have three months a year to spend full-time on the company. He describes himself as a critical and impatient boss and says things change when he's around. Sounding a bit like a crew coach, Hecht says, "I see things cluttered and not working and I kick ass." To unclutter things and make them work, he breaks them into what he calls "bite-sized tasks." "That's my contribution," he adds. "If I were to die tomorrow, the company would keep on going because of the power of the idea."

It is the idea, more than the money, that continues to entrance Hecht. He makes Books on Tape sound as if it were completely natural, inevitable. "People sometimes forget, but what we've done is restore the story to its original form of presentation through a gifted storyteller. The imposition of Gutenberg and the printing press was awful, an aberration in terms of the pure inhalation of the essence of literature."

Postscript

Books on Tape's impressive catalog of some 1,500 fiction and non-fiction titles is mailed to thousands of listeners and potential listeners around the country. A long-range planner, like most successful entrepreneurs, Hecht hopes to have 5,000 titles available by the end of the century. He admits that it might be easier and perhaps even more profitable to concentrate on best sellers, but he has opted to offer everything from Robert Ludlum to Robertson Davies, from Thomas Tryon to Thomas Hardy. Says Hecht, "The *New York Times* calls itself the 'newspaper of record.' Speeches appear in the paper in full. What I'd like to do is go after the complete work of Orwell, Churchill, and others — everything they wrote and everything written about them." He pauses, then, sounding more like a visionary than a businessman, he says, "We're doing more than just renting books. We're building a *collection*. This can be a thrilling, lifetime project."

Books on Tape, Hecht hopes, will eventually evolve into Information on Tape and serve as the depository where people go when they need something in recorded form. "It will have taken a little longer, but it will be worth it, and in the true sense of the word it will be more valuable," he says. "Not just in the monetary sense. But you can only eat so many hundred-dollar dinners in your life."

LESSONS FROM
DUVALL HECHT

1. Start small and test it. Make little mistakes that won't kill you.
2. Don't borrow money, because if you're wrong it will kill you, and if you're right your business should pay for itself out of cash flow. This is a very conservative

approach. The people at Harvard Business School and at Federal Express might laugh at me.

3. Be persistent. If you stick with a dream and it is correctly conceived, you'll succeed.

4. I remember staying up all night to redesign some sales literature. The next day a colleague told me, "You're screwing around with the periphery of the idea. You think if you choose the right color for a brochure that it will turn things around for you. You should be spending time on the core of the idea. If the central idea is powerful and right, it will carry with it a whole host of imperfections." God, that is so profound!

ELAINE COGAN
– ELAINE'S TEA COMPANY, INC. –

As Elaine Cogan's profile indicates, the innovator who can use the resources at his or her full-time job to help launch a part-time business is at a great advantage.

The Idea

To the Editor.

I have just returned from a trip to New York and other Eastern points, and was impressed (depressed may be the better description) to find once again that it is difficult to get a good cup of tea in your part of the country. . . . This may seem an insignificant matter in the cosmic scheme of things, but tea drinkers are not an insignificant part of our population, and our discomfort should not be taken lightly. . . .

Elaine Cogan
Portland, Oregon

When Elaine Cogan penned this letter to the *New York Times* in November 1983, she had no idea that she had taken the first step

114

toward establishing her own part-time business. Her hands already full running a consulting firm with her husband, Arnold, and writing books and newspaper articles, the last thing she needed was a new enterprise. But her complaint — that restaurants uniformly brought her a cup of hot water and a tea bag, that no one seemed to understand that tea needed to be brewed in a pot — mobilized America's heretofore silent minority and started a revolution of sorts. Within months of brewing trouble, Cogan had started Elaine's Tea Company, a mail-order business offering fine teas, fine teapots, and fine advice on how to prepare and serve the beverage. How did a somewhat tongue-in-cheek letter create such a tempest in a teapot? Letters to the editor of even such august publications as the *New York Times* rarely mobilize a subculture. Had Cogan's complaint been the final printed word, there is little likelihood that she would today be spending all her spare time building a new company. But when the newspaper followed up with a sympathetic editorial, circumstances were suddenly beyond Cogan's control.

"The power of the press," laughs Cogan, a cheerful woman in her early fifties. "The letters just started pouring in. Some people found my address. Others just wrote 'Elaine Cogan, Portland, Oregon.' I don't know how they found me. You had to go to a lot of work."

The letters revealed a sizable subculture of tea lovers who had suffered silently for years at the hands of what the *Times* editorial had termed "coffee bigots." These tea lovers seemed to view Cogan as a kindred soul, if not savior. They complained that they could not find a good tea, period, thanked her for giving voice to their problems, and awaited her next move. No strangers to theories of supply and demand, Cogan and her husband quickly sensed that there might be an untapped market for a tea business and set out to see if the intuition was correct.

The first thing the Cogans had to determine was what form a tea business might take. Busy running their own firm and actively involved in community affairs, the Cogans were not looking for a change of careers. Any new venture would have to blend in with their existing endeavors. "Mail order was the only thing we really considered," says Cogan. "We knew we couldn't compete in the retail market at general stores or grocery stores. Mail order was something we could do from our own office without having a lot of people — distributors, the whole network."

A Market Survey

The Cogans' next step was to determine whether there was a need or demand for such a business, whether such a venture already existed, and whether the endeavor was viable. Cogan Sharpe Cogan, the couple's firm, had done numerous surveys for clients. "We have a lot of people doing market research for us, so we decided to take a flier," says Cogan. With the luxury of using their office as a base of operations, they conducted a survey for themselves, calling targeted organizations like the Tea Institute and food editors at newspapers and magazines. The information gathered was encouraging.

"The survey was very professional," says Cogan. Questions were phrased to maintain the secrecy of the project under consideration. "We never gave ourselves away. We said we had a client interested in knowing what people were drinking." Buried among several red herrings was the question asking whether people would be interested in buying tea from a mail-order operation. The response was positive. Some people even cited Cogan's letter and the follow-up editorial. "We'd come full circle," Cogan says with a laugh.

As the Cogans contemplated their next move, they were approached by a representative of Murchies', one of Canada's finest tea companies. Says Cogan, "He showed up at the office and said, 'If you're a tea drinker, let me show you what I have.' Then he opened up a big box of sample teas." Following this, John Harney, another respected tea purveyor, sent samples of herbal teas. The quality of the teas and the companies' professed willingness to work with a fledgling operation mobilized the Cogans. "We said to ourselves, 'We have something here,'" says Cogan.

Using the Resources at the Full-Time Job

Convinced that they had something, the Cogans had to determine how to integrate this exciting, but potentially expensive and time-consuming, new venture with their other responsibilities. Says Cogan, "We decided the only way we could exist was under the umbrella of our existing business. We couldn't have done it if we hadn't had our business here. We had our office, people working for us, a secretary, no overhead for salaries or anything else. The only thing that was going to cost anything was the product."

Finding Financing

The "product" was to be a catalog offering teas and pots and cozies and other paraphernalia to make the tea-drinking experience an enjoyable one. The Cogans determined they would need $60,000 to produce and distribute the catalog. The couple could not finance the venture. "We didn't have any available cash, and we didn't want to borrow from a bank, because we didn't want to pay it back," Cogan says. Where, then, was the money to come from?

The Cogans incorporated and then sold stock in their new company. "We drafted a document that showed it might take a couple of years before we were profitable," Cogan says. "We warned potential investors of the risks. That's very important."

When looking for investors, says Cogan, "You want people who have some imagination, who'll say, 'This is a crazy idea, but it just might make it.' We approached friends, relatives, people who would have confidence in us."

Going into Production

At the urging of those who invested immediately in the company, Cogan set about producing the catalog before the full $60,000 had been raised. Cogan had consulted catalog experts, and they had advised her to have the catalog produced by professionals. Confident in her own abilities, she ignored this advice and opted to do it herself. After making arrangements with the tea purveyors and finding local artisans to supply teapots and cozies, Cogan began spending all of her spare time on the catalog. Wisely, she used the talents of the staff of Cogan Sharpe Cogan and freelancers with whom the firm often worked. The catalog was completed in less than six months. "That's a very short time," Cogan says proudly, "but we didn't know any better."

Never having produced a catalog before, Cogan had studied existing ones. She had borrowed some ideas, but had concluded that most catalogs were not very good. She felt it very important that her effort convey the spirit embodied in the original letter to the *Times,* the philosophy that had led her to embark upon the project. "We spent hours and hours setting up the pictures to create that philosophy," says Cogan. "There is a point of view that tea is for every occasion. It sets a mood."

The impressive catalog shows tea on a nightstand and on a table with tennis rackets to make the point that any time is teatime. Accompanying the pictures is a brief history of the beverage and advice on how to prepare and serve tea. The catalog has the quality of a personal letter from Cogan; it conveys the feeling that tea drinkers share a special bond. This is the Cogan philosophy, and is reflected in the company name as well. The Cogans considered other names — Quality Tea Company, A-1 Tea — but decided on Elaine's because, as Cogan says, "That's what it is, a personal service."

Marketing

In the fall of 1984, before the Christmas season, Elaine's Tea Company mailed out some 48,000 catalogs. Most of the recipients were targeted because they were on other mailing lists the Cogans had rented from a New York–based mailing list broker (yes, there are such specialists!). The Cogans took the names from seven lists that seemed relevant. "Some generated a response and some didn't," says Cogan. "For example, the Friends of Wine are not friends of tea."

At the same time, they took out advertisements in two carefully selected publications. The newsletter of the organization TeaTimers was selected for obvious reasons. The magazine *Yankee* was chosen because the Cogans reasoned that its New England–based readership was made up of many tea lovers. The newsletter proved a good choice, the magazine a poor one.

Moonlighting

How has Cogan managed to find the time for Elaine's Tea Company *and* Cogan Sharpe Cogan *and* her writing? "Making a living still takes priority over Elaine's," Cogan says, although she acknowledges that she expects the tea company to provide a handsome living in the not-too-distant future. "I've just worked hard to squeeze everything in. Luckily, being a consultant doesn't mean all work has to be done from nine A.M. to five P.M. I can do my writing and work for the clients at night and on the weekends. My clients haven't suffered, although maybe I have."

Postscript

Elaine's Tea Company's first catalog generated what Cogan calls "a credible response." Perhaps more important, it generated a great deal of national and international publicity, all of which set the stage for future mailings and catalogs. In addition to gaining the attention of magazines and newspapers, the catalog also interested members of the Portland business community. Impressed by the professionalism of the effort, several well-to-do, well-connected Oregonians have become shareholders, raising the total amount raised to over $100,000. The additional capital will help fund the introduction of a special-label Elaine's Tea that will be marketed through the mails and directly to restaurants. "All the business people we talk to say we really have something," says Cogan.

Despite the heady talk about the future, Elaine's Tea Company remains for the time being a ma and pa, and office, operation. Elaine Cogan stays up nights to write personal letters to the scores of tea drinkers who write to her. Arnold Cogan, who as a boy found work filling grocery orders, now fills tea orders before he goes to work. At Cogan Sharpe Cogan the staff enthusiastically helps with clerical and administrative tasks and assists in the sampling and selection of teas. "We all look at this as an opportunity that we'll never have again," says Cogan.

LESSONS FROM
ELAINE COGAN

1. Stay healthy, eat well, keep your sense of humor.
2. Have stamina, an extra source of income, and a lot of confidence in yourself.
3. Carve out something you can do well. This seems like it was something new for me, but remember, I'm a writer and I wrote the catalog.
4. Surround yourself with good people. Pick people you know and trust. Don't think you have to go outside your city to find qualified people.
5. Never cut corners in quality. Cut products if you have to, don't try to do as much. But don't cut quality.
6. Be honest. Feel good about the way you're conducting the business.

Entrepreneurs generally start part-time endeavors because they want to, not because they have to. As labors of love, rather than necessity, such endeavors usually capture the hearts, then the time, of their creators. Often, they become more enjoyable and fulfilling, if not more profitable, than the innovator's full-time job.

Having stamina and having good organizational abilities are two prerequisites to launching a part-time venture. Love being a great motivator, most entrepreneurs make sure they find the time to nurture their new ideas. And they make good use of that time.

Having a spouse or office to provide backup support, while not necessarily a prerequisite, certainly helps. Duvall Hecht is the first to admit that it is much easier to organize a business when your wife is looking after its day-to-day operations. And Elaine Cogan is more than willing to share the credit for her success with her supportive husband and the staff of their full-time business.

8

Making the World a Better Place: Creating and Starting a Not-for-Profit Organization

We're all going to be given an accountability. I could envision God saying, "Okay, Roskam, what did you do for society in the seventies and eighties when you had a fat job, the good life, a good family?"
— V. R. "SWEDE" ROSKAM

Great ideas need not be profit-making ideas. The business of America is not only business. The nation has long prided itself on its commitment to the underprivileged and the unrepresented. Along with government, the private sector has played a major role both in meeting basic needs and in providing basic opportunities.

As the federal government drops its "safety net" lower and lower, the private sector may have to play an even greater role. Fortunately, the recent renascence of entrepreneurial zeal extends to the not-for-profit world as well. Business people and those with little business experience alike are perceiving needs and coming up with wonderful innovations to address them.

The ins and outs of starting a not-for-profit organization could fill an entire book. This chapter is intended as an introduction to the elementary issues of the not-for-profit world. Perhaps not surprisingly, the steps necessary to turn a great not-for-profit idea into a reality are very similar to the steps required to launch a moneymaking venture.

The two profiles that follow were selected because they illustrate how people with different backgrounds — a businessman and a homemaker-volunteer — turned their great ideas not into money, but into realities every bit as important. Swede Roskam's not-for-profit Assistance Ltd. generates scholarships for hundreds of students who might otherwise be unable to attend college. The leadership of Mary Boyer resulted in the creation of a children's museum that educates and entertains thousands of Chicago youngsters.

V. R. "SWEDE" ROSKAM
– ASSISTANCE LTD., INC. –

The Institution

The concept is simple. A business agrees to donate goods (excess equipment or inventory) to a not-for-profit corporation. Then that not-for-profit corporation locates a college willing to exchange scholarships for the donated goods. The exchange is made, the business receiving a tax-deductible receipt and the college receiving the goods and issuing scholarship tuition credits to the not-for-profit middleman. Next, a student applies to the middleman for financial aid. The middleman pairs the student with an appropriate college, and after the necessary review, the student is issued a scholarship in the name of the business which originally donated the goods. "Everybody wins," says Swede Roskam, the founder of Assistance Ltd., the not-for-profit corporation that serves as a middleman in transforming everything from excess shelving and computers into education for the disadvantaged.

Years ago, Roskam was able to attend college only because a local family provided a scholarship for him. He is returning the favor. Organized in 1982, Assistance Ltd. already arranges more than $1 million a year in aid to some 200 students at more than seventy universities. "Our goal is $40 million a year," says Roskam, a bearded man in his early fifties with an outward enthusiasm and inner calm.

The enthusiasm has always been there. Since graduating from Harvard Business School in the 1950s, Roskam has been a top salesman for a number of major corporations and is currently the vice-president in charge of the Agri-Tech division at Chicago-based Oil-Dri, Inc.

The calm is relatively recent. "In 1979, there was a lot of unrest in my soul," explains Roskam. "I wasn't dissatisfied with my job, or my marriage, or my family. I was unhappy with my contribution to society."

Roskam's "contributions" to that point can hardly be deemed minimal. He had always been active in his church and was a director of the Chicago Bible Society. In addition, after the Korean War, he and his wife, Martha, had adopted and raised a homeless Korean-American infant along with their own children. Still, Roskam was restless. "I was seeing such a disparity between the haves and have-nots," he says. "I thought, 'What can I do? What can a group of us do to make a change in today's world?'"

In seeking an answer, Roskam quickly decided he wanted to start something new. Acknowledging that the zest of the not-for-profit entrepreneur differs little from the profit-making one, he says, "I wasn't interested in jumping on the bandwagon. I figured I'd search until I found something different."

The Idea

The search ended in an airplane in the fall of 1981. Roskam, who spends half his time making calls on corporate accounts, was flying back to his Glen Ellyn, Illinois home after a meeting at Union Carbide, when a *Time* magazine article on bartering caught his eye. "I'm not a ripper-outer," he says, smiling. "But I ripped this out."

The article explained that "barter," the exchange of goods or services in return for goods or services, had become a multimillion-dollar industry. Says Roskam, "I read that article and reread it. I must have looked at it over thirty times. I figured these guys who are bartering put their pants on one leg at a time just like I do. I can do this."

Do what? How could barter be employed to help the have-nots? That was unclear until a few weeks later. Driving from Chicago to visit a business in Terre Haute, Indiana, Roskam was struck with the idea for Assistance Ltd. "It was almost like a bolt of lightning," says Martha Roskam. Swede Roskam agrees: "I can remember the moment it hit me. I pulled off the side of the road and made a call to get the thing started."

The recipient of Roskam's call was Dan Mickelson, an executive with Monsanto Corporation. Says Roskam, "When you've got an idea, you should bounce it off as many people as possible." Mickelson, with whom Roskam and Oil-Dri did much business, was enthusiastic about the idea and agreed to sign on, not on behalf of Monsanto, but in an individual capacity. Soon, Roskam enlisted other friends. All had particular skills they could lend to the new enterprise; there was an accountant, a lawyer, and a handful of businessmen.

To Be For-Profit or Not-For-Profit

While Roskam was enlisting volunteers, he was pondering a critical question: Was the enterprise going to be structured as a for-profit or a non-profit-making organization? He decided on not-for-profit for a variety of reasons. "If it had been for-profit, I might have run into problems with the company I was working for," he explains. Also, Monsanto's Mickelson indicated he would only get involved if it were a not-for-profit venture. Finally, and perhaps most important, it seemed that the credibility of this type of endeavor would be enhanced if it were clear that Roskam was not going to benefit financially.

The Board of Directors; Choosing a Name

The individuals initially tapped for help by Roskam became Assistance Ltd.'s first board of directors. Selection of a board is always an important step for a not-for-profit organization. Some organizations opt for large boards composed of community leaders; these leaders are often asked to do little except lend the prestige of their name and station. Other organizations covet wealthy directors, whose principal function is to contribute money. Roskam, however, was looking for something different. "I wanted a small board, and I wanted a working board, not one in name only," he says. "I told the board members, 'I don't want your money. I want your time and expertise.'"

The board immediately lived up to Roskam's expectations, helping him refine the concept of the organization. Roskam also received input from both the academic and corporate communities in shaping the goals of what was eventually named Assistance Ltd. (The word "Assistance" was suggested by a friend, then "Ltd." was added to lend a touch of class. "Choosing a name is very important. You want something that indicates what you do," says Roskam. "It's just like naming your own child. In a sense, the organization is like a baby.")

Not-for-Profit Status, Funding, and Planning

If an organization is to receive charitable, tax-deductible contributions from individuals or corporations, it must become what is called a 501 c 3 or not-for-profit corporation. This numerical nomenclature derives from the appropriate Internal Revenue Service code provision. Shortly after New Year's Day, 1982, Assistance Ltd. applied to the IRS seeking such status.

Unable to solicit contributions until they gained IRS approval, Roskam and his board busied themselves with other tasks. Developing a pilot program was the first priority. Roskam knew from the beginning that he wanted to start small. Here, he was merely applying what he had observed in the business world. "The biggest mistake in business, for-profit or not-for-profit, is that people go off into the wild blue yonder, half-cocked," he says. "It's tempting to want to save everyone in the world overnight, but if you go in with a high-powered overhead, thinking you can do that, you're going to get into trouble. We wanted to go slowly, go full circle on a small scale and then expand it." Roskam thus resisted the temptation to solicit funds for start-up from corporations or individuals. During the first year of operation, he contributed several thousand dollars of his own to the cause.

While awaiting IRS approval, Roskam, just as an entrepreneur beginning a for-profit venture, began to target both suppliers and his market. The suppliers would be corporations which had the kind of equipment that could be bartered for scholarships. The market would, of course, be colleges. But what colleges? Roskam decided there was such a decision-making hierarchy at state schools that his program would be smothered in red tape. Private liberal arts colleges appeared better-suited. He explains, "People at the smaller schools can make decisions. Schools like Harvard and Princeton, wealthy schools with waiting lists, wouldn't need the service. But other liberal arts schools could benefit. We wanted those schools that could use the materials from the corporations and had empty seats and could accommodate students."

Market Research

Roskam determined that the best place to start small was in the area where he lived. Through both his business and community activities, he had come to know several college officials in the Chicago area. He now paid calls on these officials to see if the market existed, if the idea was as viable as he believed. The question he asked was a simple one: would the school award scholarships, in the name of the contributing corporation, in amounts roughly equivalent to the value of the donated goods? Although Roskam has since been turned down by colleges, all of the schools he initially surveyed were interested. "They said, 'I'd be a fool not to participate,'" recalls Roskam.

Starting Up

Assistance Ltd. received IRS approval in the spring of 1982, and soon began to approach potential corporate donors. How were these "suppliers" targeted and approached? Roskam hired his son Peter, a college student, to research the corporate scene and compile a list of companies that had the appropriate goods for barter. Using various reference guides available at public libraries, Peter pinpointed the companies. He then drafted a letter to the presidents of the companies. Accompanying the letter was a brochure, which Roskam and his board had spent a great deal of time designing. It included, among other things, pictures of the board members and brief biographies. "It was very important to establish credibility," explains Roskam.

The letter and brochure were sent to the presidents of approximately one hundred corporations. Roskam's experience in the business world told him that the presidents might not act upon the mailing themselves, but that they would make sure it was acted upon. Roskam had cleared his participation in this project with Oil-Dri. But he did not initially solicit his employer or the many other companies with which he did business. "We wanted to prove this could work without asking for help from Daddy," he says.

The corporate response to the letter was not overwhelming. "We got lots of Dear John letters back," admits Roskam. Some companies, however, did ask Roskam to make presentations, and one company, W. W. Grainger, Inc., based in Skokie, Illinois, soon donated $10,000 worth of air conditioners, motors, and shelving. Roskam gave half of the goods to Loyola University in Chicago and half to nearby North Park College, and Assistance Ltd. had its first scholarships to offer. "Now we had credibility," says Roskam. "It showed we had a concept and it was viable."

Operation

Roskam immediately revised the solicitation letter to indicate that Assistance Ltd. already had a successful track record ("We're always changing the letter"). On the advice of an executive who liked the idea but did not quite understand it, the brochure was also revised. Roskam commissioned a cartoon drawing that outlined the steps in the process and illustrated the benefits to the corporation. Says the brochure, "The value of the corporate donation is actually *doubled*. A $10,000 gift of materials generates the normal tax-deductible receipt *plus* $10,000 worth of scholarships for disadvantaged or needy students. Thus, a $10,000 gift is leveraged into $20,000 worth of benefits."

127

Gradually, more companies became involved, donating computers, desks, paint, and laboratory equipment. Having done it "without Daddy," Roskam soon felt comfortable approaching corporations with whom he did business. One of them, Monsanto, has donated over $150,000 in goods ranging from office equipment to a nuclear magnetic resonator. Allied Van Lines has also helped by contributing shipping services to get the goods to the campuses.

Roskam, who had quadruple-bypass heart surgery in the middle of all this, spends virtually all of his free time paying calls on corporations and speaking to gatherings of business executives. As is the case in the for-profit sector, Assistance Ltd. has become somewhat of a family affair. Peter Roskam has accompanied his father on several calls, and Martha Roskam keeps track of the books and scholarships. The board also plays an active role. "They've told me to do a few things I didn't want to do, but I've done them," says Roskam. "As my wife says, there's no use having a board if you're not going to listen to them." Still, Roskam remains the heart and soul of Assistance Ltd. In 1985, he received a special citation from President Reagan's program for private-sector initiatives.

This recognition by the government has been followed by recognition from the press. Although aware of the tremendous potential of the story, Roskam for a long time avoided trying to promote his program through the media, because he feared Assistance Ltd. would not be able to meet the demand generated by such exposure. Says Roskam, "You have to have the horses in place, because when success comes, if you're not ready, not big enough to handle it, it will be a disaster."

Postscript

Success having been achieved on the small scale originally envisioned, Assistance Ltd. is rapidly expanding. Oil-Dri has donated office space to the organization, which now for the first time has access to a computer so that inventory can be tracked. Recognizing the dramatic potential of the concept, the board decided to hire an executive director and a full-time, paid staff. Although tempted to take the executive directorship, Roskam opted to remain with Oil-Dri, which was reluctant to lose his services. He continues to chart the future course of Assistance Ltd. and to solicit corporations in his spare time. He has never been paid for this and never will be. "I wouldn't work like this for *money*," he explains, laughing. Although he is busier than ever, Roskam confesses that he has never felt so at peace with himself. "My son says I'm a little like Joshua," he says. "I spent all those years — on the road, in the business world — learning before I entered the Promised Land."

LESSONS FROM SWEDE ROSKAM

1. Find a need and see how you can fill it. Can you do something in a different manner than it is already being done? There is no sense reinventing the wheel.
2. Talk your idea over with as many people as possible and see what they have to say.
3. Start small. Creep, then crawl, then walk. Don't try to hit it big overnight. Build a history of success.
4. Good management is essential.
5. Have a working board.

MARY BOYER
– EXPRESS-WAYS CHILDREN'S MUSEUM –

The Institution

Express-Ways is not a conventional children's museum. Every exhibit is designed to involve the child. "It is learning by doing, not by passive viewing," proclaims a museum brochure. Since it opened its doors in 1982, Express-Ways has involved tens of thousands of youngsters in exhibits like "Getting to Know Hue," an introduction to the world of color; "Amazing Chicago," a mini-city of architectural wonders; and "City Hospital," a behind-the-scenes look at the world of medicine. The museum also serves as a resource center, with workshop courses for teachers, and offers special workshops for school groups and families. Included in this smorgasbord are mime, creative writing, and x-ray art.

Whereas Assistance Ltd. is the result of one man's vision, commitment, and energy, Express-Ways is the result of the collective efforts of public educators, the Junior League of Chicago, and private citizens. How the idea for the institution was transformed into an explosion of sights and sounds and smells and touches is best presented by profiling one of those private citizens, Mary Boyer.

The Idea

The seed for Express-Ways was planted in 1978, when Mary Boyer was appointed to the Arts Advisory Committee of the Illinois State Board of Education. A 1968 graduate of Northwestern University's journalism school, Boyer had worked in advertising for Montgomery Ward before leaving to raise a family on Chicago's North Shore. "I'm not an activist," she says. "But I grew up in a family that encouraged participation in community affairs, and I've always been interested in the arts."

The committee's mission was to promote a state plan that would encourage quality arts experiences in the public schools. "Unfortunately, that plan came along at just about the same time that funding for the arts was being cut," says Boyer. This lack of money, combined with the inertia that often characterizes advisory boards, resulted in little action for over a year. Gradually persuaded that the committee would never have a significant impact, Boyer began to consider other alternatives for bringing arts to the schools. What motivated her? "Maybe it was that even though I went to fine schools, my education in the arts was deficient, and I wanted my children and other children to have a better experience."

Enter the Junior League of Chicago, a volunteer organization that trains young women for leadership in the community. Boyer had been a member since the middle of the 1970s. Aware that she did not have the resources to spread the arts to schoolchildren throughout Illinois by herself, Boyer immediately thought of the Junior League, which was already involved in programs with the Chicago Symphony

Orchestra and the Art Institute of Chicago. "The league's best record was in the arts and education," she explains.

Boyer bounced this notion off fellow Junior League member Jeanette Kreston. Kreston, an accomplished musician, agreed there was a role for the league, and the two set about planning a program that would further schoolchildren's participation in all the arts. Soon a Junior League committee had been formed to help with planning and research.

Planning and Research: Part One

The first step was to determine the nature of the program. This research was virtually identical to that undertaken to determine the direction of a for-profit endeavor. Boyer, Kreston, and others in the league visited people involved in running existing institutes for the arts and talked to arts educators. They also established contact with other community-based organizations. "At this stage," says Boyer, "our plan was to do something in the schools, probably a model school project." A closer look at the Chicago public schools dissuaded her. "The situation there was so volatile that we didn't think we could do a three- to five-year model project," she says.

Boyer's research suggested an alternative. Included in material she had received from the National Endowment for the Arts was a description of a children's museum in Denver. "That intrigued me," she recalls. "We didn't have one in Chicago." She called the museum's director, who in turn put her in touch with Suzanne Cohan and Jean Unsworth, two Chicago educators interested in starting such a museum in the city. Coincidentally, it was Cohan and Unsworth who had written the report that led to the formation of the committee on which Boyer had served. In the spring of 1980, Boyer and Kreston met with the educators. "We learned that their concept was unique, different from existing children's museums," says Boyer. "They envisioned interactive exhibits for kids where they actually did things. Then, what the kids learned in the activities was reinforced through workshops." Boyer was excited. "I felt, 'This is it,'" she says. "The idea was sound and had the possibility of reaching a lot of children. Working through the schools would have taken much longer." Boy-

131

er's enthusiasm was matched by Cohan's and Unsworth's. "They were excited because the Junior League had money and volunteers to get the thing rolling," Boyer says.

A Difference of Opinion

Success in the not-for-profit field, as in the for-profit field, rarely happens overnight. Despite such enthusiasm, it would be more than two years before the great idea was a reality. While the educators and the Junior Leaguers agreed on the validity of the core idea, there were other areas in which agreement was harder to come by. "We had a great deal of difficulty with the division of labor, determining who would do what and who was in charge," says Boyer.

The speed at which the project should move was also an issue. The educators were, understandably, anxious to see their concept in action, but Boyer and her colleagues, aware that the name and the resources of the Junior League were at stake, were more cautious and businesslike. "I felt a feasibility study was square one," says Boyer. "We had to find out how much it would cost, if the money was available, if it would work." Cohan and Unsworth, with true entrepreneurial spirit, wanted to leapfrog the study, purchase the mammoth, and vacant, Dearborn Street train station, and begin operation. "They had huge plans," Boyer says. "But I didn't think we had the finances or administrative ability to run something like that."

Such policy disagreements are common in the business world, and their resolution is essential if an enterprise is to work. Boyer and the Junior League eventually prevailed on the issue of a feasibility study, because, as Boyer acknowledges, "We had some leverage because we were the ones coming in with the money."

It should be noted that, at this point, Boyer had yet to ask the organization for any funding. She was waiting to play her cards until the right moment, realizing that the approach should be made when she truly needed the money. "I felt we could do the planning and the feasibility study on a voluntary basis," she explains. By now Boyer and Kreston had been joined in the volunteer effort by Marilyn Eisenberg, a creative thinker and tireless worker.

Planning and Research: Part Two

Prior to conducting the feasibility study, Boyer and her colleagues had researched children's museums in other cities and determined that approximately $600,000 would be needed to launch their venture — a museum with exhibits, workshops, and a theater. The Junior League was certainly not capable of providing all of that. Where would it come from? "Not the government," says Boyer. "The handwriting was on the wall that the government wouldn't be funding the arts." The corporate world seemed a logical source of funds, but would Chicago's business community support the idea?

The feasibility study was a good way to find out. Designed by Junior League members who had expertise in the planning field, the study questionnaire asked two basic questions: Is there a need? Do you think we could raise $600,000? "We were careful not to ask for money," says Boyer. Junior League volunteers took the questionnaire to a carefully selected group of business and community leaders, educators, and funders. By the middle of 1981, the results were in. Most of those surveyed thought there was a need for the museum. Most also thought that $600,000 sounded like a great deal of money. No one surveyed came forward and offered to participate financially. In addition, Boyer sensed that some of the other museums in the city were less than cooperative about encouraging the creation of a new institution.

Finding Financing

It was time to look for money. In the fall of 1981, Boyer asked the Junior League to contribute $50,000 for each of two years to provide a financial basis for the endeavor. This plan is similar to what entrepreneurs do, putting up their own money in good faith before seeking it elsewhere. If the innovator is not willing to take a risk, why should anyone else? The Junior League money would not have to be given immediately, however. "We said we wouldn't actually ask for it until we had matched it from other sources," says Boyer, "because we weren't sure we had our act together. We felt if we had money immediately, we'd be under pressure to rent space and secure equipment and exhibits, and we weren't ready to do that."

Over the next several weeks, the Junior League volunteers sought financial support from the community. None was forthcoming. Economic times were bad and corporate giving was reduced, but still, Boyer admits, she resented the lack of commitment. "Everyone was saying we had a great idea, but that they couldn't help," she says. "This was our low point." Boyer was beginning to feel the heat from the educators and from within the League. "I was stuck," she recalls.

Planning and Research: Part Three

She remained stuck until she decided to examine more closely how other children's museums had started. "People had told us during the feasibility study that we should start small," Boyer says. "And then I learned that the museum in Pasadena had started with one exhibit."

Now believers (like Swede Roskam) in the notion that small is better, Boyer and the planners distilled the museum into its essential elements. They dropped the more ambitious plans for a theater, concentrating on the exhibits and teacher training. Urban Gateways, a Chicago community organization, agreed to do the training, while the Junior League and the educators concentrated on the exhibits. Or rather, the exhibit. "We decided to start with one exhibit," says Boyer, who figured that they could persuade someone to donate the space for such an exhibit to run for three months. She was right. The Chicago Public Library's Cultural Center donated two unused hallways. "We started by hoping for Dearborn Street Station and settled for two hallways," she says with a laugh.

Starting Up

It was now the spring of 1982, over a year since the Junior League and Cohan and Unsworth had joined forces. A plan was finally in place: an exhibit would open in the fall. "We called it a pilot program, so even if it fell flat on its face, it would be worth it," says Boyer.

Now the Junior League money would come in handy, but no matching funds had been raised, and to get the money immediately would require a revote by the membership. Fortunately, the League agreed to count the in-kind services donated (the Cultural Center space and supplies) as money and contributed the promised funds. Boyer decided not to seek money from other sources at this point — a source of debate with the educators — but, says Boyer, "We now figured we'd have a better chance once the program got going."

Board of Directors

A board, however, was necessary immediately. "We wanted people with an interest in the arts who had high profiles," says Boyer. Professional fundraisers and Junior League members helped compile a list of desirable candidates. They wanted no more than ten directors initially and wanted a mix of workers, people with money, and people with prestigious names.

Prospective board members were solicited with confidence. "By now we had it knocked," says Boyer. "People were impressed by our tenacity. And we told them, 'We need you, but it's going to happen without you.' We went to them quite proud of our accomplishments."

While prospective board members were being approached, plans were being made for the exhibit. The planners had considered renting an exhibit, but eventually decided to create their own — "Getting to Know Hue." "It was all coming together," says Boyer. The next task was to let their audience know they were going to be in business. Boyer and the other founders held meetings with local school principals and sent out a brochure to schools. Initially, the plan was to staff the museum with volunteers from the Junior League, but because the exhibit was to be in a library hallway, the planners soon realized that someone would have to be there at all times.

"It was too early to go out and get a top-notch executive director," says Boyer. "We didn't think anyone would quit a job to work with us at this stage. But we did need paid help." Eventually Kreston and another woman were hired to watch the exhibit, coordinate volunteers and tours, and run the office.

The problems that arose now were good problems. Demand was so much greater than anticipated that a system had to be designed to handle the requests of school groups wishing to visit the exhibit. "The phone didn't stop ringing," says Boyer.

The exhibit (preceded by what Boyer describes as "a splashy lunch for the board") opened on October 15, 1982, and within three weeks additional help had to be hired. By January 1, Boyer and the planners knew they were going to have a successful program. They also knew that with an additional $50,000 promised by the Junior League, and brighter prospects for other funding, it was time to look for an executive director. They were able to persuade their first choice, Dianne Sautter, a teacher and development director, to leave her job to join the new venture. "Once that was done, I felt my job was over," says Boyer, who was the first president of the board.

Postscript

The operation of Express-Ways remains a collective enterprise. Under Sautter and Kreston (now assistant director), Eisenberg (who assumed the board presidency after Boyer), and Cohan and Unsworth (who have remained as paid consultants), the museum has flourished. Boyer is still involved, too. In this era of government cutbacks, she is looking for ways for the museum and other not-for-profits to generate funds so that they can become self-supporting. "The word *entrepreneur* is not a contradiction in the not-for-profit field," she says. "An entrepreneur is someone who finds new ways of solving problems and follows them."

LESSONS FROM MARY BOYER

1. Be sure about who is responsible for what aspect of a project. If you have a group, it is best to define roles from the beginning.
2. Develop a plan, but remain flexible and adaptable and be able to change gears.

3. Set up controls that will tell you if it's going to be successful. This process is similar to starting up any business venture.
4. Know your limits or capabilities based on funding, personnel, and time.
5. Have a larger vision, but begin on a scale you can handle and control.

The steps necessary to turn a great not-for-profit idea into a reality are virtually the same as those needed to transform a for-profit idea into a successful enterprise. The profiles of Swede Roskam and Mary Boyer illustrate that those who approach social issues with entrepreneurial zeal and intelligence can indeed make the world a better place. Not-for-profit entrepreneurs may have one advantage over many of their for-profit brothers and sisters. They often have the luxury of starting small and proceeding slowly. If there is one lesson to be learned from Assistance Ltd. and Express-Ways, it is that pilot programs can help the not-for-profit venture fly.

Part 2

TURNING YOUR IDEA INTO A REALITY

9

Nuts
and Bolts:
a Recipe for
Success

It's a personal thing. The business is me. It represents
what I stand for, who I am, what I am, and why I am
what I am. It really drives you. You can't say no. You
can't give up.

— WILLIAM HORNIG

Something exciting is happening. The marketplace is beginning to
teem with wonderful new ideas for products, services, and establishments. Why? The revivification of the general economy, the explosion in technology, changes in the work force, changes in values —
these and other recent events have created a climate in which Alfred
North Whitehead's pursuit of adventure plus Samuel Butler's pursuit
of profit equals entrepreneurship.

Entrepreneurship itself, of course, is not a new idea. Americans
have always taken pride in their inventiveness and daring, and the
nation's economic and social systems owe much to the pluck of the
late-nineteenth- and early-twentieth-century risk-takers and profit
seekers. But at some point that pluck seemed to give way to corporate conservatism. Managers, while properly viewed as important,
became dominant, usurping the role of explorers and creating a ster-

ile, if not stagnant, workplace. There were too many Indians and not enough chiefs.

As proof that the law of supply and demand usually corrects such imbalances, the chiefs have begun to come forward. As the profiles in the previous chapters reveal, they are an interesting and diverse lot. People who a decade ago considered *business* a dirty word are now bringing their energy and values to the marketplace. Many who thought they had neither the time nor talent to go into business are now finding that their life experience and common sense are invaluable assets when starting a new venture. And some who thought the only way to success and happiness was to start climbing from the bottom rung of the corporate ladder are now finding much greater fulfillment setting up their own ladders.

As the profiles also indicate, setting up such ladders — turning a great idea into a reality — is not always easy. If there is such a thing as an "overnight success," few of these individuals are aware of it. Many entrepreneurs believe that coming up with a great idea is the easiest part of the process. "Great ideas are a dime a dozen," says Brett Johnson, who dropped out of Harvard College in the late 1970s to sell painter's caps imprinted with customized logos. "You have to do something with the idea." Johnson's company, Crowd Caps, Inc., eventually grossed over $7 million annually, but it took several years of knocking on doors and living on a shoestring budget before the idea was rewarded.

Johnson acknowledges that, "A lot of times, I just flew by the seat of my pants," and still marvels that he landed on his feet. Many people with great ideas are not so fortunate. They end up crashing to the ground because they fail to apply sound judgment and good business principles to their ventures. Before taking off, then, the innovator should sit down and create a flight plan.

You have a great idea. Now what? Or, in less kind terms, so what? What basic steps should you take if you want to turn your idea into a viable enterprise?

The process consists of five phases:

1. Evaluating your idea
2. Creating a business plan
3. Structuring your business

4. Finding financing
5. Starting up

PHASE ONE: EVALUATING YOUR IDEA

"At the time, it seemed like a great idea." This epitaph can be found on the tombstone of many a venture that died an early death. It is true. At the time the light bulb of creation flashes on, a feeling of elation, of boundless optimism takes hold of the innovator. This sky's-the-limit mentality is often quickly reinforced by spouse or friends, who either know little about the particular idea envisioned or are too polite to burst the loved one's bubble. Giddily, then, the crew imagines fame and fortune. *People* magazine and the rest of the paparazzi will be camped on the doorstep. The money will roll in, paying for the kids' college educations, the new kitchen, the trip or new car.

Perhaps. But before committing a great deal of time and energy and money to the effort, it is essential to emerge from the self-congratulatory euphoria and objectively evaluate the idea. You must ask two questions: Is my idea truly viable? And do I have the desire and resources to follow through on it?

Is My Idea Truly Viable?

Kip Fuller, the Denver-based inventor whose creations have included both winners and losers, offers one method for evaluating a new product idea: "Create a prototype, and then visit your neighbors and see how they react. If you call on ten, and five of them won't immediately write you a check for the product, think twice. They may tell you it's great, but they're probably reacting like family, appealing to your ego. If you can sell them, then maybe you have the real thing."

Too many innovators fail to sit down and determine whether their idea will appeal to anyone beyond the bedroom walls. As Fuller says, "They generally don't ask themselves the hard questions. And if they do, they cheat when answering. It's more fun that way. But the exhilaration of that moment may be matched by the depression they feel later on."

You must weigh a number of factors in evaluating your idea's viability. First and foremost, there should be a need. Your idea should have inherent appeal, for if you have to manufacture or generate such interest — with the exception of certain fad or novelty items — your venture is almost surely doomed.

There are several ways to determine need. Fuller's approach may work for some skilled people wishing to introduce a new product, but something else is required for those envisioning a new service or business establishment. A market study may provide the answer. While you can hire marketing specialists to conduct such studies, they are usually expensive. Money for their services may be well spent at a later planning stage, but at this point in the process most entrepreneurs choose to conduct their own "surveys." Thus, Duvall Hecht sent a trial-balloon letter to the members of an affluent local organization, asking if there would be any interest in cassette recordings of books. And Jeffrey Ullman took off his wedding ring and attended numerous singles' functions to ask if video dating made sense.

Unfortunately, need alone does not guarantee the viability of an idea. There may be a need for the product, service, or business you envision, but, unknown to you, someone else may already be satisfying it. Before proceeding too far, then, it is important to discover whether there is any competition. The presence of others in the field is not necessarily fatal. It does, however, require that you seriously consider whether your mousetrap will be able to compete against existing mousetraps. If it is better or at least different, or you have some other unique skill or advantage, there may be no problem. If, however, a company with more expertise and capital has cornered the market, you should seriously reevaluate. For example, the presence of competitors forced Michael Cullina and Steven Byer to open their salad bars in Philadelphia rather than Boston.

Just because there is no competition when an entrepreneur enters a market or begins production does not guarantee that competition will not arrive shortly. Small imitators looking for a quick buck and sizable companies with greater resources frequently come in after new waters have been tested. The first company into a new field generally enjoys an initial competitive advantage, but in evaluating long-range prospects, you need to consider whether your company can withstand the entry of significant rivals.

Survival may depend on the ability to protect the great new idea. Ideas in and of themselves are not patentable. Indeed, they are extremely difficult to protect in any manner. Products and processes, on the other hand, may be patentable. The ability to secure such protection may be an important factor in considering whether or not to go into business. If it is, read the following section. If not, you may want to skip ahead to the section on resources for evaluating an idea.

Patents

In an effort to encourage creativity and foster a fair and efficient marketplace, the federal government affords legal protection for some inventions. This protection takes the form of an exclusive property right to an invention, or patent. Issued by the Commissioner of Patents and Trademarks, U.S. Department of Commerce, a patent gives an inventor the right to exclude others from making, using, or selling an invention for seventeen years. A patent is different from both a copyright (which protects literary and artistic work) and a trademark (which protects a product's name or symbol). Trademarks are regulated by the Commissioner of Patents and Trademarks, while copyrights are administered by the Copyright Office, Library of Congress, Washington, D.C.

Just because a patent can be secured, does not mean it should be. The process is long and costly, and even if you're successful, you may find yourself sued for infringement by the holder of a similar patent. Inventor Fuller gives another reason for thinking twice about getting a patent. "It's important to patent hi-tech products," he says. "But for the typical product, your best protection is to access markets as quickly as possible. The money spent on getting a patent may be better spent on marketing and distribution to ensure a big market share at the beginning. *That's* how you discourage competition."

What Is Patentable?

Ideas cannot be patented. Thus, novel as it was at the time, Jeffrey Ullman's idea for a video dating service was not protectable. What *is* patentable? According to the federal government:

1. Any new, useful, and unobvious process (primarily industrial or technical); machine; manufacture or composition of matter (formulas, for example); or any new, useful, and unobvious improvement thereof
2. Any new and unobvious original and ornamental design for an article of manufacture (*Design patents* differ from regular patents in that they are applicable for three and a half, seven, or fourteen years, as the applicant elects.)
3. Any distinct and new variety of plant, other than tube-propagated, that is asexually reproduced

What Isn't Patentable?

1. An idea (as opposed to a mechanical device)
2. A method of doing business (for example, the assembly-line system)
3. An inoperable device
4. Printed matter (a copyright may afford protection)
5. An improvement in a device that is obvious or the result of mere mechanical skill

Securing a Patent

If you want a patent, there are several steps you must follow. After getting the idea for a product, you should:

1. Make certain the idea is practical and profitable. There is probably little sense in worrying about a patent if there is no need or use for the product envisioned or if production would not result in monetary gain.
2. Write down the idea, describing what is original and patentable

and how the product is superior to any similar products which may already be on the market and patented. Write down the idea in a way that provides legal evidence of its origin; the procedure should be witnessed, dated, and signed by a friend. (This may prove important in establishing a claim at a later date. It is a good idea to keep a good record of the entire process.)

3. Establish that the product is novel. This is a two-step procedure. First, the product should be analyzed to determine whether it meets the standards for patentability described above. Second, a search must be conducted to determine whether or not a patent already exists. The search room at the Patent Office in Arlington, Virginia, just outside Washington, contains records and descriptions of the over four million patents issued in the United States and more than twice as many foreign patents. Until recently, the inventor either had to travel to Arlington to conduct the search or retain an attorney or search firm to do the research. A third alternative now exists: there are over thirty "depository libraries" in public libraries around the country with the facilities for conducting searches. A list of these libraries can be obtained from the Patent Office.

4. Apply for the patent. This assumes, of course, that the search did not reveal a similar patent. A patent application includes a written document that comprises a petition, a specification (description), and an oath; a drawing where possible; and a filing fee. It may take as long as two years for an application to be reviewed.

Expert Counsel

Patent procedures can be detailed and complicated. Therefore the SBA, most established inventors, and others with an understanding of this field strongly encourage the innovator to seek counsel from experts and have the application drafted and filed by a patent attorney or agent. Such professional assistance is not inexpensive. A patent attorney involved from the beginning of the process may charge several thousand dollars. Agents, such as the invention promotion firms, are also costly. You will have to pay these fees whether or not your application is successful.

Only attorneys (or agents) who have registered with the Patent Office can prosecute an application. The office will provide a geographical or alphabetical listing of these individuals, but will make no recommendations. Word-of-mouth is probably the best way to find good counsel.

Your first visit to a patent attorney should be exploratory. It is important to establish that the attorney understands both you and your idea. As most patent attorneys have engineering backgrounds, there should be few technical problems; the attorney may even be able to help find additional technical assistance if necessary. Try to solicit an honest appraisal of the chances for securing a patent. A good lawyer or agent should try to discourage the innovator with an obviously unpatentable item from proceeding.

A Final Note

Be advised:

- If you have described the product in a printed publication or used it publicly or put it on sale, you must apply for a patent before one year has gone by; otherwise the right to a patent is lost.
- Marking "patent pending" on a product after applying for a patent has no legal protective effect.
- The free SBA pamphlet *Introduction to Patents* served as a resource for this discussion and is an excellent starting point for patent-seekers. The Government Printing Office's booklet *General Information Concerning Patents* is also helpful.

Resources for Evaluating an Idea

Would that there were a toll-free hotline to answer questions for the person with an idea. In the meantime, there are sources that can help you determine the viability of your ideas. You can get advice from governmental agencies, not-for-profit organizations, and private, for-profit corporations.

The federal agency which can offer the best counsel is the SBA.

Having survived both funding cuts and the efforts of some politicians to eliminate it altogether, the SBA still has offices in several regions of the country. These offices offer direct counseling services, sponsor inexpensive workshops on getting started in business, and provide referrals to other governmental and private-sector resources with expertise in particular fields. (See the Resource Guide at the end of the book for a listing of regional SBA offices.)

Don't be surprised to find that the SBA and those sources in its network are very cautious about the prospects for success. Because of the high failure rate of new ventures, the agency tries to impress upon the advice-seeker the perils of entrepreneurship.

The SBA also publishes a number of pamphlets with information geared to those thinking about going into business. These pamphlets, authored by SBA officials or experts from the private sector and academia, provide valuable advice and often include extensive lists of other resources. Most of these publications are available free of charge. Beyond the SBA, there are other governmental agencies that can provide direct assistance or referral aid to anyone trying to evaluate an idea. Contact your mayor's or governor's office for more information.

Many universities have formal programs designed to evaluate new ideas and provide assistance to innovators, and the SBA sponsors Small Business Development Centers in conjunction with some colleges. Most of these programs are free or entail minimal expense. Contact the SBA for more information, or call your local or state university (see the Resource Guide for a list of some university programs).

Offering programs similar to these university centers are the growing number of inventors' associations and councils. Most are not-for-profit, and when there is a membership fee it is nominal. Many provide workshops and "bull sessions" at which budding innovators can share their thoughts (see the Resource Guide).

In the private sector you can retain lawyers, accountants, management and business consultants, and marketing experts to help you evaluate your idea. However, these specialists, whose services are often costly, may prove more beneficial at a later stage in the process.

"Invention promotion firms" also provide evaluation, marketing, and brokering services to those with new product ideas. Typically, such a business will charge a fee of several hundred dollars to prepare a marketing report that evaluates the prospect of a product. If the marketing report proves favorable, the firm will then undertake to find a manufacturer for the product. This can save you a good deal of time and effort. The cost for this service may run to several thousand dollars even if a manufacturer is never found, and if the promotion firm is successful it will take a significant portion of your royalties.

While many of these firms are no doubt reputable and can even boast of success stories (the post-hole digger was apparently produced in this fashion), the government, patent attorneys, and professional inventors urge the neophyte to exercise extreme caution. An SBA pamphlet, *Can You Make Money with Your Invention?*, cites a Federal Trade Commission investigation which found that one firm, charging fees ranging from $1,000 to $2,000, was successful on behalf of only 10 of its 35,000 clients. The ratio at another firm was even lower: of 30,000 clients, only 3 met with success. Says Kip Fuller, "Generally speaking, these brokers are raping their clients. They're just salesmen who take the money up front. They take advantage of people in a euphoric state of mind."

The SBA will urge you to request solid evidence about the firm's track record and verifiable statistics on the number of clients represented and the number who have actually made money. You should also check the firm's reputation with your local Better Business Bureau, a patent attorney, or local inventors' association. The SBA recommends avoiding firms that collect the entire fee in advance.

Do I Have the Desire and Resources to Follow Through?

There may be a need for your new product, service, or establishment. There may be little competition in the field. Still, unless you are willing and able to follow through, the idea will, like milk on the shelf, eventually sour.

William Hornig worked sixteen hours a day, with no time off and no other help, during Solar Wash's first several months of operation. Turning an idea into reality generally demands such dedication . . . and stamina.

When asked why they went into business for themselves, many entrepreneurs respond that they were seeking a freedom they could not find at their desks in corporate America. They wanted to be their own bosses. Now on their own, they have learned that the boss works harder than anybody else in the organization. Says Re-Creations' Marcia Goldberger, "When you work for a large company, you have more flexibility to take a kid to a doctor's appointment or music lesson than when it's just you manning the store. On your own, it's a twenty-four-hour workday. That means if I want to go to a grocery store in the middle of the day I can. But then I have to tag it on at the end. That's not good, is it?"

For the person who wants to start a full-fledged business, the effect of this venture on spouse and children is a serious consideration. The Snugli enjoyed its first wave of success when Mike Moore began paying personal calls on parent and childbirth organizations across the country. Moore, who explains that the purpose of promoting Snugli was to promote better parenting, soon appreciated a certain irony in his own circumstances. He was on the road so much that he was missing out on the parenting of his own children. A family conference resolved the conflict. "We decided we weren't going to let the business disrupt the family," Moore remembers.

Along with the absence of parents, the presence of inventory and other business material in the home can also be disruptive. When Coralee Smith Kern started Maid to Order in her home, she annexed her son Kevin's bedroom for an office and he had to move in with his sister. Lynn Tatar laments that during peak candy months her product, packaging, and ingredients cannot be contained in the kitchen and eventually fill every room in the house. "Even under the bed," she sighs.

Entrepreneurs and families make adjustments, and the desire to follow through on an idea is often strong enough to overcome the knowledge that hard work, financial sacrifice, and the disruption of the household are inevitable. If you know what you're getting into and still want to go ahead, you must next consider whether you have the resources to succeed; namely, time, skill, and money.

Few entrepreneurs or business consultants would recommend that you make time for a new venture by immediately quitting your present job. This drastic measure may never be required, but if it is, it should be preceded by a great deal of planning. Remember, Duvall Hecht was working full time in the investment field and teaching crew while he developed and nurtured Books on Tape. He claims he learned an important lesson from a popular play and movie. "In *Mr. Roberts*," Hecht explains, "someone says the navy is a system designed by geniuses to be administered by idiots. I don't mean to sound arrogant, but in a sense Books on Tape is a very simple idea, and if you keep the simplicity of the idea throughout its operation — if you don't shoot yourself in the foot while executing it — it will be clean and uncluttered and very easy." You can also save time and money if, as Elaine Cogan did, you can use the resources at your present job — secretaries and other personnel, telephones, supplies, business contacts.

With her background in business, Cogan already possessed the basic skills and experience necessary to turn her idea into a company. Many innovators are not so fortunate and must therefore decide while still evaluating the idea whether they will give up, bungle ahead by trial and error, acquire the requisite skills, or find someone with those skills. Little needs to be said about those who give up. In many cases, discretion may be the better part of valor.

Few entrepreneurs recommend the trial-and-error method, agreeing instead with Michael Cullina's advice to get experience in the field you're thinking about entering. Cullina, you will remember, did learn about his prospective trade by working as a waiter at a salad bar, but he says he would have benefited even more if he had enrolled in a major restaurant chain's management training program. "Like most entrepreneurs, I was too impatient," he confesses.

Cullina succeeded, but sometimes limited experience is too limiting. Some ventures simply demand organizational or technical skills beyond the innovator's capability. The nonengineer, for example, who has an idea for a better mousetrap is going to need help in drawing and building a prototype. It is during the idea-evaluation phase that you must determine whether such help can be supplied by another individual or entity. While some patent attorneys and the inventors' councils and university-based enterprise forums may be of help here, most prospective entrepreneurs appear resourceful enough to make the determination on their own. They generally consult family, friends, other entrepreneurs, even the Yellow Pages, to find the missing pieces to their puzzles. For example, although Ann Moore conceived of the Snugli, she needed her mother to help her design and make the prototype.

What if you have a great new idea but don't have the desire or the resources to follow through by actually starting a new business? It is not impossible to see the idea come to fruition by selling it to an existing business. But it is difficult and often frustrating.

SELLING AN IDEA

We're the Braintrust — a company whose sole purpose is new product development. We make ideas work for a living. And we put that philosophy to work for clients on purely conceptual projects; developing ideas for new products or services; or new ideas for existing products or services.
— FROM PROMOTIONAL LITERATURE, THE BRAINTRUST

It sounds like a great idea in its own right. The Braintrust was, as its literature continues, "a group of highly creative people . . . with an average of 15 years' experience in the new product development area . . . [offering] bright ideas." Dial the telephone number listed on the promotional literature today, however, and a recording announces that the number is no longer in service.

Talk with Mike Morris, the sincere and knowledgeable graphic designer whose brainchild the Braintrust is, and he announces that it was far more difficult to sell ideas than he had imagined. The Braintrust came close on several occasions — a big contract with a toy company was almost signed; a major cereal company expressed interest in an idea for a promotion; a publishing company considered an idea for a guide to parking in Chicago. But, in the end, nothing materialized with these companies or virtually any other company that the Braintrust approached.

Morris formed the Braintrust after working as a designer for a major corporation for several years. The other members of his consortium brought similar experience in different creative fields to the task. With their extensive backgrounds in the corporate world, these people knew how to market their services in creative fashion, how to target corporations that could use those services, whom to approach at those corporations, and how to approach these decision-makers. Still, the noble experiment failed. Why?

The cynic might suggest that the ideas the Braintrust offered were simply not good enough. Morris, of course, offers several different explanations. Primary among them is that most corporations do not even want to consider ideas from outsiders. But aren't new ideas the lifeblood of our economic system? Shouldn't corporations do all they can to seek out the new and innovative? Yes, the corporations answer. And that is why we have hired our own talented people to come up with new ideas — people who know our system, know what we want and how we want it. Frankly, continue many corporations, the ideas we get from outsiders are so seldom suited to our purposes that it makes little sense to devote our resources to evaluating them in the hope that one might prove valuable. Moreover, the fear of being sued by an individual who claims we stole his idea — even though we may have been working on the same idea on our own for several years — is a strong deterrent against considering *anything* from unknown outsiders. If we are going to look outside the corporate walls, it will be in the direction of established inventors and designers with track records, most preferably track records with us.

This stream of (corporate) consciousness is hypothetical, but accurately reflects the sentiments of several corporate officers interviewed for this book. Many of those companies that would seem best suited to ideas from outside innovators — food companies (ideas for a new product), television production companies (ideas for a series or script), toy and game manufacturers (ideas for a new product), and advertising agencies (ideas for a new campaign or promotion), are among the most reluctant. Corporations in these fields (and in other areas as well) believe the solicitation and evaluation of new ideas from nonprofessionals is simply not worth the time and money and potential legal wrangling. The toy manufacturer Coleco is an exception. For several years, the company has considered ideas from everyday people who are not professional toy designers. The results are hardly encouraging; in all those years, the company has yet to purchase an idea from such a source.

Coleco's record, the Braintrust's experience, and the apparently dismal success rate of the invention promotion firms must give the layman pause. In most cases, the person who is not a professional inventor or designer can do very little with an idea. The only way to see that idea become a reality and, perhaps, profit from it, may be to create the product and go into business.

Still, for the person who cannot or does not wish to start a new business, Chaucer's six-century-old admonition may apply: "He that naught n' assaieth, naught n' acheveth." There may be nothing to lose in sallying forth to sell the idea itself. What is involved in such a venture?

The Basic Steps in Selling an Idea

The steps here parallel to a great degree those for selling a new product directly or starting a new service or business establishment.

1. You must determine whether the idea is a viable one.

2. You must determine what corporation or other entity would have the greatest use for the idea. This may be a hit-or-miss operation. Friends, relatives, and corporate contacts may be helpful in providing direction. In addition, a survey of similar products already on the market should lead to the doorsteps of suitable manufacturers. A trip to the public library may also prove beneficial. Most "business" sections contain reference books listing companies by product line. Among the best references is the *Standard Guide to Advertisers,* a listing of over 17,000 corporations. The corporations are listed by type of product sold.

3. You must determine what the targeted company's policies are with respect to considering ideas from outsiders. This should be relatively easy to ascertain by telephone or letter. The *Standard Guide to Advertisers* also lists the officers of each corporation. If there is a Vice-President for New Product Development or something similar, this is probably the best person to query. If there is no such listing, the switchboard operator should be able to direct the caller to the responsible person. If that fails, go right to the top and ask for the president of the corporation. His or her office will be able to make the proper referral.

4. You should attempt to protect the idea as much as possible

before revealing it to a company. Ideas alone cannot be patented. Protection, therefore, may be difficult. Before revealing an idea, the innovator should request that the company sign what is commonly called a "nondisclosure agreement." Under such an agreement, the company promises that it will not divulge the idea or make use of it without compensating you. It may be advisable to have a lawyer draft such an agreement.

Unfortunately for the innovator, few companies will sign such an agreement. Instead, before agreeing to look at a new idea, a company will require the innovator to sign a form holding the company harmless in the event the company does make use of the idea at some later date. Why? It may be that the company is already researching and developing the same idea. Such an agreement serves as protection from lawsuits by individuals claiming the idea was stolen. The innovator thus finds the deck somewhat stacked. Because the company holds all the cards, it is the company that will probably end up with legal protection. If the entrepreneur is not willing to divulge the new idea under these circumstances, the venture ends here. Most entrepreneurs seem willing to proceed, trusting that a reputable corporation would not risk its good name to steal an idea from an individual. That trust is usually well-placed.

5. You should present the idea to the company in a professional fashion. Sometimes you can make this presentation in person. More often, however, the company will want to see something written before meeting. The presentation should be neatly typed and accompanying diagrams should be neatly drawn. A description of the idea should be included; the market for the idea should be outlined; if known, the projected costs and benefits of proceeding with the idea should be detailed. If you have conducted any preliminary research, that, too, should be included.

6. You should follow up. Recognize that you are probably not one of the company's top priorities. Follow-up letters and phone calls generally are required just to get the responsible person to consider the idea.

And if the company should want to purchase the idea?

7. You and the company must agree on a price for the idea. It may be difficult to determine the value of an idea in and of itself. Fac-

tors to be considered would include how much time and money you have spent generating the idea and the monetary value of the idea to the company. Compensation may take the form of (1) a one-time flat fee for the idea, or (2) a royalty based on an agreed-upon percentage of the sales. There are advantages and disadvantages to each of these forms. The flat fee may make the innovator feel more secure. Even if the idea flops, the innovator will have money in hand. On the other hand, if the idea is a huge success, the innovator may regret not having taken a percentage of the sales. The best arrangement may be a combination of the two forms: a flat fee advanced against royalties. Here, the innovator is guaranteed some compensation and can also participate if the venture takes off.

PHASE TWO: CREATING A BUSINESS PLAN

Great Expectations' Jeffrey Ullman remembers the scene well. Soon after being struck with his great idea, he visited his parents. Heavy on enthusiasm and confidence, but light on specifics, he asked them for several thousand dollars so that he could start a video dating service. They turned him down. "They said, 'Hell, no.'" Ullman laughs. "But if you present us with a business plan, we'll fund you.'" Ullman spent the next several weeks developing such a plan, then returned to his parents, and persuaded them of both his and the idea's seriousness.

Although it may come as unwelcome news to many would-be entrepreneurs who, impatient to begin, find details boring and unnecessary, transforming an idea into a viable enterprise requires planning. One suspects that Jeffrey Ullman's parents demanded a plan not so much for their benefit as for their son's. Your new venture is probably doomed if you are unable to think through *and commit to paper* the major aspects of starting the business. A business plan forces you to establish goals and to consider how the enterprise will operate. Only with planning can opportunities be identified and exploited, resources allocated, problems anticipated, strategies designed, logical decisions made. And, if all that is not enough, only with a plan can you reasonably expect to persuade lenders or attract investors.

The extensiveness and sophistication, the form and content of plans will vary from business to business. Marcia Goldberger produced a minimal plan because she was already familiar with the retail clothing business and knew that she was going to finance her venture with her own money. On the other hand, entering uncharted waters and in need of financing, Solar Wash's Hornig produced a detailed plan with comprehensive strategies and projections.

These examples suggest that while the primary purpose of the plan is to force you to think about the business, you should also tailor it to its intended audience. Friends and relatives who might invest in a project will probably not want the same information that venture capitalists or bankers will demand. Similarly, graphics, flow charts, and product or plant diagrams may be necessary in some cases and superfluous in others. In all cases, however, the language should be clear and as free from technical jargon as possible, and you should avoid the temptation to paint the rosiest picture possible. Business plans are generally read with healthy skepticism. If you disclose potential problems, you may do more to impress prospective investors than if you deny any risks.

Although a business plan for a new product may differ from one for a new service or establishment, there are certain items that should be considered for all plans:

1. State the goals of the venture.
2. State specific objectives and present a timetable for accomplishing those objectives.
3. Describe what products or services will be offered and whether there are any considerations with respect to patents, copyrights, or trademarks.
4. Discuss the competition.
5. Detail the competitive advantages of the venture — the superiority of management or the product, the price advantage.
6. Describe the target market and its potential.
7. Discuss trends in the industry.
8. Present a marketing strategy that includes plans for market penetration, pricing, sales, and distribution.

9. Present advertising and promotion strategies.
10. Describe the production process, if relevant, including sources of material and labor requirements.
11. Describe the site selected for the venture.
12. Detail the structure of the organization and how it will be managed.
13. Discuss employee and space requirements.
14. Present an operating plan for the next six months to three years and detail start-up and research and development costs.
15. Provide and explain financial projections for at least three years, including profit-and-loss and cash flow statements.

While this list may seem intimidating, most of these concerns are really quite basic. You should be able to define your goals, describe the business, outline marketing strategy, plan management, and consider financial implications. Again, the depth with which these items need to be examined will vary from business to business. If little depth is required, you may be able to do the entire business plan by yourself; it may be only a page or two. If more detail is required, you may need to engage an accountant or lawyer to help, particularly with the financial data. As well as producing the business plan, these professionals can help you set up a bookkeeping system and structure the business. To locate a reputable professional, ask friends or relatives or other entrepreneurs.

The initial meeting with a lawyer or accountant should be used, among other things, to determine whether a comfortable relationship can be established. The professional may ask you tough, but helpful, questions about the viability of the business. Frequently the professional will consider this a "getting-to-know-you" session and won't bill you. This is the time for you to ask questions, too. What services can the professional provide? How much will those services cost? Don't feel embarrassed to ask about fees. Most good lawyers and accountants expect and encourage such discussion. Often, when a business is just getting started, a lawyer or accountant will offer services at a reduced rate. If these fees are still beyond your means, the SBA may be able to provide relief. The bar associations and accountants' associations in many states also offer free assistance.

PHASE THREE: STRUCTURING YOUR BUSINESS

The structure a business takes should be contingent on the short-term and long-term needs of the project. There are important tax and non-tax factors to be considered. Among the questions to be weighed are:

1. What is the risk, the investor's liability for debt and taxes?
2. What would happen to the firm if something happened to the principal or principals?
3. Which structure allows for the desired administration of the firm?
4. What are the possibilities of attracting additional capital?
5. What are the costs and procedures involved in starting?

There are four basic structures: a sole proprietorship; a partnership (limited or general); a corporation; and a Subchapter S Corporation.

Sole Proprietorship

This is the structure most often selected by individuals starting new businesses. It is generally defined as a business completely and directly owned and operated by one person. To create a sole proprietorship, you need only obtain whatever licenses, if any, are necessary to begin operations; few legal formalities are required to start, and it is usually less expensive to establish than a partnership or corporation. The sole proprietor, as sole owner of all assets, is entitled to all profits, but must also shoulder all of the venture's liabilities and operational losses. The major sources of funding are the proprietor's personal assets, the money generated by the business, or borrowing.

A business can begin as a sole proprietorship and then be changed to another structure. Maid to Order's Coralee Smith Kern and Snugli's Ann and Mike Moore are typical of many entrepreneurs. Starting small and funding themselves, they chose to operate initially as sole proprietorships. But as business boomed, liability increased and tax and financing considerations became more complex. These sole proprietors eventually decided to incorporate their enterprises.

Partnership

This structure is usually defined as an association of two or more persons carrying on as co-owners of a business for profit. Some partnerships are based upon oral understanding, but most are created by formal agreement. Although the individuals in a partnership have joined forces for a common, profit-producing motive, a partnership is not considered a separate legal entity from the partners. A partnership, therefore, may not be sued in its firm name only; instead, each partner shares potential liability.

There are two basic types of partnerships. A *general partnership* provides that each partner shares in the firm's profits and losses either equally or in some agreed-upon ratio. Under normal circumstances, a general partner has unlimited personal liability, including assets outside the business. A *limited partnership* consists of a general partner and limited partners, so called because their liability is limited to the extent of their capital contributions.

Partnerships, particularly limited partnerships, are well suited to ventures that have a short (or at least defined) life expectancy, such as the marketing of novelty or fad items.

Corporation

William Hornig's assertion that "the business *is* me" must be qualified. Individuals form corporations because that structure ensures that the business, from a legal standpoint at least, *isn't* "me." In a landmark 1819 Supreme Court decision, Chief Justice John Marshall wrote that a corporation "is an artificial being, invisible, intangible, and existing only in contemplation of the law."

A corporation, then, is a legal entity distinct from the individuals who own it. As a separate entity, it can sue and be sued, generally act in its own name, even hold and convey property. Its rights and powers derive from state statutes and its own articles of incorporation and bylaws. And, perhaps most important to many entrepreneurs, creditors may not look outside the corporation for the satisfaction of business debts.

Subchapter S Corporation

This structure combines most of the elements of a corporation with one very important element of a partnership. As in a partnership, profits and losses of a Subchapter S Corporation flow directly to the individual shareholders. This option is particularly attractive to entrepreneurs anticipating losses during the initial stages of operation, because shareholders have the benefit of offsetting those business losses of the corporation against their personal income. The decision to become a Subchapter S Corporation is not irrevocable. Typically, after investors use initial losses to reduce their personal tax liabilities, they drop the S status and the firm becomes a corporation, taxed at the lower corporate rates.

Selecting the best structure for a new enterprise is extremely important. Following, based on the SBA pamphlet *Selecting the Legal Structure for Your Firm,* is a breakdown of the advantages and disadvantages of each structure.

SOLE PROPRIETORSHIP

Advantages

1. Ease of formation
2. Sole ownership of profits
3. Control and decision making vested in one owner (There are no coowners or partners to consult, except possibly a spouse.)
4. Flexibility (Management is able to respond quickly to business needs in the form of day-to-day management decisions as governed by various laws and good sense.)
5. Relative freedom from government control and special taxation

Disadvantages

1. Unlimited liability (The proprietor is responsible for the full amount of business debts, a sum which may exceed the proprietor's total investment. This liability extends to *all* of the proprietor's assets, such as house and car. Additional problems

of liability, such as physical loss or personal injury, may be lessened by obtaining proper insurance coverage.)

2. Unstable business life (The enterprise may be crippled or terminated upon the illness or death of the owner.)
3. Less available capital, generally, than in other types of business organizations
4. Relative difficulty in obtaining long-term financing
5. Relatively limited viewpoint and experience (This is more often the case with one owner than with several.)

PARTNERSHIP

Advantages

1. Ease of formation (Legal expenses and formalities, while greater than sole proprietorship, are few compared to requirements for corporation.)
2. Direct rewards (Partners are motivated to apply their best abilities by direct sharing of the profits.)
3. Growth and performance facilitated (In a partnership it is often possible to obtain more capital and a better range of skills than in a sole proprietorship.)
4. Flexibility (A partnership may be more flexible in decision-making than a corporation, but less so than a sole proprietorship.)
5. Relative freedom from government control and special taxation

Disadvantages

1. Unlimited liability of at least one partner (In the case of a limited partnership, the general partner would have such liability. The insurance considerations detailed in the discussion of sole proprietorships apply here, too.)
2. Unstable life (The elimination of any partner may constitute automatic dissolution of the partnership. However, operation of the business can continue based on the right of survivorship and possible creation of a new partnership.)

163

3. Relative difficulty in obtaining large sums of capital
4. The firm can be bound by the acts of just one partner (acting in agency capacity for the partnership).
5. Difficulty of disposing of partnership interest (The buying out of a partner may be difficult unless specifically arranged for in the written agreement.)

CORPORATION

Advantages

1. Limitations of the stockholder's liability to a fixed amount of investment
2. Ownership is readily transferable.
3. Separate legal existence
4. Stability and relative permanence of existence (For example, in the case of illness, death, or other loss of an officer or owner, the corporation continues to exist and do business.)
5. Relative ease of securing capital in large amounts and from many investors
6. Delegated authority (Centralized control is secured when owners delegate authority to hired managers, although they are often the same.)
7. The ability of the corporation to draw on the expertise and skills of more than one person

Disadvantages

1. Activities are limited by the charter and various laws.
2. There is the potential for manipulation and exploitation of minority stockholders.
3. Extensive government regulations and required local, state, and federal reports
4. Less incentive if a manager does not share in the profits
5. Expense of forming a corporation
6. Taxation (There is, in effect, a double tax. Corporate profits are taxed and individual salaries and dividends are also taxed.)

An understanding of the different natures of the four basic options provides an excellent theoretical starting point. Conversations with other entrepreneurs about their practical experiences are also helpful. Often, however, the technical and financial factors involved are complex. To avoid making a wrong or costly decision, it may be advisable to consult an attorney or accountant.

PHASE FOUR: FINDING FINANCING

After Elaine Cogan had reached the happy conclusion that there was great demand for a mail-order tea business and that she had the expertise to operate such a business, she had to face a not-so-happy reality. "The one thing my husband and I didn't have was money," she recalls. "We were very smart. But we didn't have any available cash."

Cogan eventually found financial backing. Without any capital, of course, a new venture is virtually impossible to launch. Moreover, without *sufficient* capital, a business is almost certainly condemned to failure.

You should project the financial requirements of your new venture when drafting your business plan. Before committing your own assets or before attempting to attract outside funding, you must know how much money is needed and for what purposes. You should also determine how long the money will be needed and how you will repay any borrowed or invested funds.

There are many potential funding sources. These sources include the entrepreneur's own assets, friends and relatives, other individual investors, commercial lenders, government programs, and venture capitalists.

The Entrepreneur

Many entrepreneurs are prepared and willing to fund all or part of a venture built around their new ideas. In most cases, some financial participation by the innovator will be necessary. Almost all commercial lenders, as well as most individual investors, will want you to participate as a sign of good faith.

In many cases, the issue is not whether the innovator will provide funds to start the new venture, but whether the innovator will be the sole source of funding. As a young man, Duvall Hecht watched helplessly as his father's large investment firm went bankrupt. The experience left Hecht extremely wary of the so-called benefits of leveraging — borrowing money to finance the operation and growth of an enterprise. When Hecht started Books on Tape, he was determined to avoid going into debt. "If you make mistakes with your own money, you get bruises," he says. "If you make mistakes with somebody else's money, you get killed."

For a variety of reasons, many entrepreneurs are reluctant to look beyond themselves for funding. Some, like Hecht are aware of all the pressures inherent in starting a new venture and do not want the added worry of repaying a loan, whether that loan comes from a bank, friends, or relatives. Others, aware of the potential for profit, do not wish to share that profit with other investors. Still others, aware of the potential for failure, are afraid to ask friends or relatives or outsiders to invest (as opposed to loaning) money.

If you have enough of your own money to risk, there may be no need to involve outside institutions or individuals. Here the definition of "enough" becomes critical; you may have sufficient funds to begin operation, but if the venture built around a new idea is severely undercapitalized, it stands a good chance of failing to take full advantage of its uniqueness, or of failing altogether. In this case, if you are truly serious about succeeding, you may have to overcome the fear of finding outside funding.

Friends and Relatives

Elaine's Tea Company was launched because friends who had faith in both Elaine Cogan and her idea invested in the venture. Saladalley became a reality because the parents of its cofounders each loaned

$20,000 to their enterprising sons. It stands to reason that those who know and love an innovator are often willing, if they can, to provide financial support by either buying shares in the firm or loaning money. To the entrepreneur with no other funding possibilities, such participation is a godsend. But there is one major drawback. If the venture fails, the relationship between funder and fundee may be jeopardized. Many an entrepreneur has spent sleepless nights worrying about losing the stake provided by dear ones, and many friends and family members have stayed up worrying about the same thing. If the stake is lost, it could cause embarrassment, resentment, or the dissolution of an important personal relationship.

You must advise a potential lender or investor of the financial risk of a venture before any money changes hands. With a friend or relative, it is wise to consider and discuss the nonpecuniary possibilities as well. For example, at one point Gordon and Carole Segal's search for $10,000 reached a friend's doorstep. Gordon Segal remembers, "He told us that if we failed, then he'd be unhappy because he'd lost his money, and that he'd probably resent us. And that if we succeeded, we'd resent him because here he was sharing in the profits while we were working our tails off." They decided that the friendship was more important than the capital, and the potential partner did not invest.

Other Individual Investors

While some new ventures require so much capital that stock is immediately offered to the general public, most businesses begin on a smaller scale. Still, you may have to seek funding from individuals who do not qualify as friends or relatives. Sometimes you will find outside investors by word-of-mouth, and sometimes outside investors will find you. Brett Johnson has recently begun to publish a newsletter that allows innovators to "advertise" for financial backing and other assistance.

Investors may want to become limited partners or shareholders in your corporation. Presentation becomes very important in soliciting the involvement of outside investors. While friends or family merely have to be sold on the idea, outsiders have to be sold on both the idea and you, the innovator. You may also have to offer an outsider a greater return than friends or family, as was the case with Kip Fuller and his robot.

Sometimes innovative financing is as important as an innovative product or service. When Gerald Guice started his Sentinel Computer Services, Inc., in Oakbrook, Illinois, he was unable to work out a satisfactory arrangement with either banks or prospective individual investors. He eventually approached prospective customers. "We told them we were going into business and asked if they would invest in us," Guice explains. No one would. One businessman, however, advised him how he had started his own service business. Guice took this concept and ran with it. The ingenious plan was this: Any customer who prepaid for five months of service would get a sixth month free. Guice would personally guarantee the contract, so that even if his business failed, the customer would be protected.

Two companies agreed to the plan, providing some $35,000 for start-up. "That really wasn't enough," says Guice. But he worked for very little until the company was on its feet. Guice also provided $11,000 of his own money.

The company survived its first months, and soon was running at a profit.

Commercial Lenders

"A banker," says General Comet Industries' Owen Ryan, "is a guy who gives you an umbrella on a sunny day." While banks might appear an obvious source of funding for ventures built around new ideas, Owen Ryan speaks for most of the entrepreneurs profiled here when he describes banks as conservative institutions which are unwilling to risk their money on innovators and innovations. Marcia Goldberger agrees with Ryan, and adds that if the innovator happens to be a women, the bank seems even more reluctant.

Banks may not be so eager to enter into such ventures because the risk of failure is high and returns are limited. Says a banker who prefers to remain anonymous, "If a bank makes a loan, it doesn't matter if the business earns ten million dollars or one dollar. The bank gets the same amount of money back — the loan repayment plus interest."

Many large commercial institutions will consider making loans only to new ventures which have fixed assets or real estate to pledge as collateral. Smaller banks in need of business may be more willing to loan. Still, these smaller banks will almost always require the personal guarantee of the innovator or a cosigner. Translation: if the assets of the new business are insufficient to repay the loan, the bank may attach the personal assets you pledge.

Entrepreneurs who have had success securing loans stress the importance of finding someone at a bank who understands the nature of a particular venture. Crate & Barrel's attempt to borrow money to finance expansion was unsuccessful, until, says Gordon Segal, "we found a banker who understood the retail business." Finding such a person may be difficult. "Bankers know money, not operations," sighs William Hornig. Hornig was able to borrow money from a bank to start Solar Wash because the business had fixed assets — washers and dryers, solar collectors — and because he pledged personal collateral. Some months later, he attempted to secure another loan for expansion. Five banks, including his original lender, turned him down. Says Hornig, "I thought for about three days and figured my logic was better than theirs; they just didn't understand what I was doing. So I called each of them back and told them I wanted someone authorized to loan $100,000 to come out and see the operation. All five came, and all five, after seeing the place, agreed to loan the money."

Whenever Hornig approaches a bank, he presents them with a comprehensive business plan projecting expenses, cash flow, and profits. Such a plan is virtually a necessity. Although some of her business practices are unconventional, Julie Brumlik had in hand a detailed budget when she sought her first loan of $2,000 for Scarlett Letters. "I think I had every expense projected to the penny," she laughs. "The typesetting machinery, the rent, even the light bulbs." Brumlik received the loan. "I think they trusted me."

Government Programs

In some cases, the SBA will make direct loans to new business ventures. Other federal and state direct-loan programs also exist. Many, however, are restricted to certain categories of applicants. The SBA also guarantees loans made by community banks. While most banks are conservative with their own money, they are a little more liberal with the resources of the federal government. The salad days Michael Cullina and Steven Byer now enjoy are a result of the SBA, and an SBA-guaranteed loan also enabled Snugli, Inc. to carry on. These loans take more time to secure than conventional business loans, and, predictably, there is much paperwork involved. Such inconveniences, however, appear minor compared to the benefits. Contact the SBA or a local bank if you are interested in learning more about the direct and guaranteed governmental loan programs.

Venture Capitalists

Most venture capitalists have little interest in becoming involved with new businesses that require less than several hundred thousand dollars for start-up. Most innovators with new ideas, save those in the high-technology fields, don't require that kind of money and won't find funding through the venture capitalists' services. Still, it's worth knowing what they do.

In short, venture capitalists find or directly provide money, and in many cases managerial assistance, so that new ventures may be launched. Often such money goes into research and development. Venture capitalists, although risk-oriented, are very particular about where they put their money. A comprehensive business plan is a necessity, and the better the track record of the entrepreneur, the better the chance of attracting funds.

In return for their services, venture capitalists generally receive a percentage of the equity in the new venture. If the business fails, the venture capitalists lose their money; if the business succeeds, they get their money back and much more. Too much more, according to some entrepreneurs, who say the percentage demanded by these funders — it can range from 10 percent to upwards of 50 percent of equity — is too high. These entrepreneurs also complain that venture capitalists often usurp control of the business's decision-making process. Venture capitalists argue that they generally only become involved in management if it is necessary to protect their substantial financial stake in the project. If you choose to enlist funding from venture capitalists, you must decide what portion of equity and control you are willing to give up and what the alternatives are. Sometimes 50 percent of a large pie is preferable to 100 percent of a small pie or no pie at all.

PHASE FIVE: STARTING UP

It is the premise of this book that you will learn best how to turn a great idea into a reality by examining how successful entrepreneurs did just that. The profiles in the preceding chapters focus heavily on the start-up phase. Still, a general review of the major steps involved in actually starting up should help you. These include:

1. Consulting attorney, accountant, and insurer
2. Meeting government requirements
3. Manufacturing the product
4. Marketing the product, service, or establishment
5. Distributing and pricing the product
6. Promoting the business

Consulting Attorney, Accountant, and Insurer

The legal requirements that will affect the business should be evaluated before the business opens its doors. Some entrepreneurs, through their own devices or with the help of others, are able to evaluate these requirements for themselves. Some may be able to set up bookkeeping and a financial control system for the business. Many entrepreneurs, however, prefer to consult with attorneys or accountants, to make sure that nothing has been overlooked and avoid any unpleasant surprises. If a new product or invention is involved, you may have already consulted them. At this stage, you will want to discuss some or all of the following: contracts, leases, employee relations, product liability, and taxes.

Many businesses are required to carry some forms of insurance, such as workers' compensation. Other types of insurance, particularly liability insurance, may not be required, but are generally advisable. In the case of a sole proprietorship or partnership, such a policy may protect the entrepreneur from losing personal assets. In the case of a corporation, such a policy may protect the firm's assets. There may be a number of other types of coverage which you should also consider, and you should apply the same care to finding the proper insurer and policies as to securing a lawyer or accountant. You will find trade associations valuable in a number of areas, including insurance. The associations frequently offer special policies and rates to their members.

Meeting Government Requirements

Different municipalities and states have different requirements for starting a business and different agencies to administer those requirements. The office of the Secretary of State (headquartered in the capital of each state) is a good place to learn about such requirements. For example, if a business is operating under an assumed name, it must register that name with the state of incorporation.

Local ordinances might also require that particular types of businesses, for example those working with food, be licensed. The federal government also has regulations. For instance, a federal Employer Identification Number (obtainable from the IRS) may be necessary for tax purposes.

Again, you may be able to survey and comply with all of these requirements without counsel; it will certainly be less costly, initially, at least. Whether this turns out to be money well saved can only be determined by future events. You could regret this decision if you are confronted by a governmental agency and charged with failure to comply.

Manufacturing the Product

Unless an idea is sold outright, a product must actually be produced; a service must actually be offered; a business establishment must actually be opened.

How do you find a source capable of manufacturing a product if you cannot produce it yourself? Sometimes, as in the case of the Snugli, innovators don't have to look any farther than family or friends. Other times, finding a producer may test your resourcefulness. When Ellen Giller decided to market her unique designer sweatsuits for children, she thought that she and a friend-partner could make the clothes themselves. Demand for the product became so great so quickly — Giller's annual sales are well into six figures — that a speedier operation became necessary. Searching the Yellow Pages (a surprisingly good source), Giller found a sewing company that was willing and able to produce large quantities of the sweatsuits. The relationship worked beautifully until the sewing company's owner, a somewhat militant Iranian, found out Giller was Jewish. Production suddenly ceased. Giller overcame this crisis with true entrepreneurial inventiveness and boldness: "I waited on the corner across the street from the company until the company's best seamstress came out," says Giller. "She barely spoke English, but I managed to explain to her that I'd pay her twice as much as the company did if she'd come and work directly for me. And she agreed."

When the Yellow Pages or a street corner are insufficient, a trip to the public library may become necessary. Library "business" or "reference" sections offer many sources of information and feature numerous aids for the beginning business person. In particular, the *Thomas Register of American Manufacturers* is a multivolume work that lists the manufacturers of various products. (Entrepreneurs manufacturing their own products will also find this helpful, for it lists sources of materials.) Trade associations may also be able to make referrals to producers. Finally, university-based enterprise forums and inventors' associations also provide guidance. Indeed, some inventors' associations will actually produce the innovation.

In the case of a service, the "product" is, in effect, the labor provided by those working for the business. Often, particularly when a firm is getting started, the entrepreneur provides all of this labor. When Great Expectations opened, Jeffrey Ullman interviewed those seeking dates, videotaped the interviews, facilitated the matchmaking, and did virtually everything else all by himself. "I lost about twenty pounds just running back and forth from the reception area to the office," he says. When the task is beyond your capability or energy, you can generally find additional help by word of mouth, by advertising, or through employment specialists.

The "product" of a business establishment is what it sells — food, clothing, tableware — and the place in which it sells it — restaurant, department store, storefront. You can generally find suppliers, wholesalers, and manufacturers, both for goods to be sold and the furnishing of the establishment, through other entrepreneurs in the same field, trade associations, the Yellow Pages, and the trusty *Thomas Register.*

In the case of specialty items for a new venture, you may have to rely on your own wits. Remember, Gordon and Carole Segal initially found the unique items sold in Crate & Barrel by contacting Chicago-based Scandinavian trade representatives and asking for suppliers.

Marketing the Product, Service, or Establishment

To whom are you going to sell — wholesalers, retailers, individual consumers? Is there a particular geographic market or type of customer? How do you target and reach and satisfy this customer?

Marketing specialists and other consultants can conduct surveys and do research to answer these questions. But their services are often expensive. Most entrepreneurs, extremely cost-conscious during the start-up period, conduct their own informal research or merely follow their intuition. If they do use marketing experts, it is generally after the venture has been launched.

The value of the information generated by the specialists or by the entrepreneurs themselves is subject to debate. Snugli, Inc.'s initial advertising campaign in *Parents* magazine, you will recall, failed miserably. On the other hand, Elaine Cogan's professionally conducted research correctly forecast the potential popularity of a tea catalog, and her use of specialized lists for a direct-mail campaign resulted in an above-average response.

Also successful were the marketing efforts of Jeff Webb, the founder of the Universal Cheerleading Association, which sponsors cheerleading camps across the country. Webb's initial strategy is instructive for its simplicity. First, he targeted cheerleading advisers as the group most likely to influence young cheerleaders to attend cheerleading camp. Second, he went to the public library and found a listing of American high schools. Third, he designed an impressive color brochure about his new camp. And fourth, he sent brochures to the attention of cheerleading advisers at hundreds of high schools, asking the advisers to pass the information on to their charges.

Distributing and Pricing the Product

You know the target audience and you know how you want to sell your product (by direct mail, through advertising, or in retail outlets). But how are you going to accomplish such sales? How are you going to get your product to your audience?

You can accomplish distribution in a number of ways. In the case of, say, a mail-order business, you may wish to operate on your own. If so, it is necessary to determine how and where inventory will be stored, who will ship it, and how often the shipping will take place. When Leland Wilkinson first started Systat, Inc., sales were modest and distribution relatively easy. Wilkinson simply stored the software and the accompanying manuals in his basement. When orders came in, he or an assistant would box the material, then journey to the post office and ship it out. When the business blossomed, Wilkinson hired more assistants and made arrangements for daily pickups by United Parcel Service. Eventually he needed a larger space for storing inventory.

Because demand was so great, Wilkinson could afford to have more space. Many entrepreneurs, particularly those in the mail-order business, are not so fortunate and are condemned to forever keeping inventory in the home. For years, the walls in Duvall Hecht's home *could* talk and *did* have tales to tell. They hosted hundreds of books on tape.

If you are wholesaling a product, you must also figure how you are going to reach the targeted audience. Brett Johnson paid call after call on college bookstores and other retail establishments that seemed logical outlets for his painter's caps. Johnson sometimes dropped in to the establishment without warning; on other occasions, he identified the manager or buyer responsible for such a product and tried to make an appointment. Much time and aggravation can be saved by such planning.

Johnson, like many other entrepreneurs, also attended gift and trade shows which bring buyers, manufacturers, and distributors together under one roof and facilitate communication and sales. Trade associations, retailers, and entrepreneurs in related fields are excellent sources of information about such shows.

Johnson spent over a year traveling around the country, knocking on doors. If you do not have the time, energy, or desire to handle distribution by yourself, distributors and manufacturer's representatives or agents can be helpful. If convinced of a product's viability, such middlemen will undertake to get the product into the proper outlets. You can make various fee arrangements with these middlemen. Distributors will often buy the product outright at wholesale or lower-than-wholesale prices and then resell to retail outlets. Representatives or agents, who do the kind of legwork Brett Johnson was doing for himself, usually are paid a commission based on a percentage of sales.

Be careful to select an effective and honorable distributor or representative who has experience with a similar product. To find a reputable middleman, ask a retail outlet which sells related products. Trade associations, other entrepreneurs, and the book *Macrae's Verified Directory of Manufacturer's Representatives* (available at most libraries) are also excellent sources of information.

Before setting a price for a product, you must know how it will be distributed. Consider a product sold in a store. In all likelihood, it was sold by the producer-entrepreneur to a distributor, who then marked up the price and sold it to the store, which marked up the price again and sold it to the consumer. Consider the same product as a mail-order item sold directly by the entrepreneur. Although there will be increased costs attendant to such self-distribution, you will often be able make the same or greater profit by selling the product for more than the wholesale price charged to the distributor, but less than it would cost in a store.

Price is a reflection of the cost of material and labor that goes into producing and presenting a product or service, the forces of competition, and the profit desired by the entrepreneur. There are basic formulas for determining the price of goods and services. These formulas may be found in business texts or through accountants and other specialists.

Independent souls that they are, many entrepreneurs ignore the formulas and price their goods or services intuitively. Leland Wilkinson's software program required minimal material (disks and printed material), but was the result of hundreds of hours of Wilkinson's calculations. How was a price to be set? There was little competition in the field, so Wilkinson was on his own. He admits that he rather arbitrarily set the price at $200. Soon, it was apparent that the market would bear a higher tariff (a competitor, entering the field after Wilkinson, charged $900 for a less comprehensive program), and Wilkinson raised the price to $500. Then, he learned that university personnel, a major source of orders, need not fill out requisition forms for their superiors when purchasing material costing less than $500. Wilkinson, therefore, lowered the price a few dollars.

Promoting the Business

Your business is now ready to open its doors. How do you let the world know? Many times, the world simply finds you. Saladalley opened with no advance advertising or publicity, and Crate & Barrel and Great Expectations ran a few small newspaper advertisements; Marcia Goldberger made sure her maternity shop was in the Yellow Pages before operations began.

All of these businesses, and many others discussed in this book, eventually attracted the attention of the press. This is not surprising. Newspapers, magazines, and the electronic media are always searching for the new and unique, and many businesses built around novel ideas fit this bill. By means of a well-considered public relations campaign, the savvy entrepreneur may be able to gain a great deal of media coverage. Such coverage is, in effect, free advertising. A half-page advertisement in the local newspaper or a national magazine may cost thousands of dollars; a half-page article (generally extolling the new idea) costs nothing.

If you want to gain the media's attention, you have the option of running your own public relations campaign or hiring an expert to do so. Again, such experts may be costly, and the entrepreneur watching expenses at start-up time may be reluctant to gamble that dollars spent on a consultant will generate even more dollars' worth of publicity. A compromise may be possible. You may be able to persuade a consultant to take a small percentage of equity in the venture in return for orchestrating a publicity campaign.

If you handle your own publicity, you should be aware of one important rule: the publicity must be well timed. If the demand for goods or services generated by a magazine article or television appearance cannot be met, the publicity will be of little financial value and may even antagonize prospective customers. Thus, even though he was aware that Assistance Ltd. had great potential for news coverage, Swede Roskam waited patiently until the operation was running smoothly before meeting the press.

Television does not have the only networks for promoting a business. Membership in trade associations or other organizations — networking — is an effective means of spreading the word, and less conventional approaches like those of Julie Brumlik can also make a splash.

This chapter has attempted to provide an orderly overview of the steps necessary to take an idea and turn it into a viable enterprise. In the real world of the innovator, such orderliness is seldom found (perhaps this is one of the reasons the entrepreneurial life lures so many). Phase two and phase three, for example, may overlap. Phase five may precede phase four.

This chapter may be best read as a recipe. There are several ingredients that go into the entrepreneurial process. It is important to *evaluate the idea* (to determine the viability of the product and your desire and ability to produce it) and to *create a business plan* (formal or informal, depending on the audience); you must also *select a legal structure* for the business; *finding financing* is essential; and, finally, the various elements of actually *starting up* (professional consulta-

178

tion, meeting government requirements, production, marketing, distribution, and promotion) must be added. In many cases, the order in which some of these ingredients are added to the mixing bowl matters little — as long as they are added.

Accompanying this recipe has been advice on where to find certain of the ingredients. The SBA remains one of the best clearing houses for general information and can often refer you to those providing specialized services. Other government agencies, universities, trade associations, professionals, inventors' councils, the public library, and other entrepreneurs can also help, and you should use them when necessary. Remember, almost every entrepreneur profiled advises: take advantage of your strengths, but recognize your limitations and engage the help of those who are strong where you are weak.

In all cases, the recipe should conclude, "Season to taste." No two innovators follow the same steps in the same order. Nor should they. Different ideas require different approaches, and different individuals have different ways of approaching challenges.

Whatever your approach, I guarantee you will find the process exciting. Now that you know how to turn your idea into a reality, read on to learn how it feels.

10

An Innovator's Journal

Marvin Rosenblum, the keeper of the little black book, says that sometimes he wakes up in the middle of the night so excited that he cannot go back to sleep. I know the feeling. More than a few times have I awakened with "great" ideas that set me to pacing until morning arrived. Some of these ideas did not look so great in the light of day, and, my head a bit clearer, I was able to dismiss them with little difficulty. Others seemed promising for a period . . . perhaps until lunchtime anyway! I would classify my idea to bronze marathon shoes in this category. Still others survived the entire day and another and another. This being the case, I had little choice but to pursue them. I have had varying degrees of success and failure with these pursuits.

My first venture was SaveCard. A college classmate and I persuaded numerous businesses near our campus to give students a 10 percent discount. To get the discount, the students had to present a special card. To get the card, the student had to purchase it from us. This was a popular item for a while, particularly with freshmen.

My next venture was a documentary film of the 1980 National Wheelchair Games. I had never heard of the event and had never worked in the film medium. But when I learned several hundred incredible wheelchair-bound athletes would be competing in track and field and weightlifting competitions, a documentary seemed warranted. I managed to raise $35,000 in a short time, secure the rights, and, with the help of skilled technicians, produce the film. It was an artistic, if not financial, success — portions were shown on network televison.

The work in film led me to try to persuade my fellow attorneys that they should make much greater use of videotape in courtroom trials. The medium and the venue were perfectly matched, a partner and I reasoned. Videotape could help the litigator show the jury that which could not physically be brought into the courtroom — accident and property sites, accident re-creations, scientific experiments, even taped theories of cases. I like to say that we didn't get in on the ground floor of this business, we got in at the basement. Most attorneys were simply not ready for the service. Despite intense marketing, the venture was only moderately successful until artistic differences and other interests split the partnership and ended the effort. The lesson here: timing and a good partner are essential.

At about the same time that attorneys were respectfully saying, "No, thank you" to the videotape service, major retail establishments were respectfully saying "No, thank you," to another idea I had: "Suds, Dial–A–Soap Opera." Inspired by a friend's storylike message on her answering machine, I was convinced that every American sitting in an office would telephone a central number day after day to hear an ongoing original soap opera. The three-minute recording would be sponsored by a retailer, who would, I figured, be delighted to reach an audience heretofore inaccessible during working hours. After much fun (a week's worth of scripts were written and several first-rate Chicago actors helped produce a pilot tape) and minimal expense, I concluded that this was an impossible undertaking.

I am happy to report that my latest venture, the subject of this chapter, has been an artistic and financial success. On a cold February morning in 1985, I awoke at about five o'clock with the phrase *The Last Yupper* on the tip of my tongue. Immediately I pictured a poster that would "contemporize" Leonardo da Vinci's masterpiece, *The Last Supper*. Who better to sit at such a table today than yuppies, young upwardly mobile professionals? Unable to go back to sleep, I had the good sense not to rouse my wife, Sharon. But when she awoke a couple of hours later, the first words she heard from me were, "The Last Yupper." She was a quick convert, and the project was off and running.

I had already begun writing this book at the time — perhaps that is what inspired the idea. As I moved forward with both projects, it occurred to me that while the profiles presented an accurate picture of the trials and tribulations involved in pursuing an idea, they did not fully convey the tide of emotions experienced by anyone who engages in such a pursuit. On any given day, an innovator is (a) convinced the idea will make him or her a millionaire, (b) convinced the idea is totally worthless, and (c) both of the above. In an effort to provide the would-be entrepreneur with a picture of this emotional roller coaster, I soon started a journal chronicling the ups and downs of DaVinci Productions, Inc., the company we formed to produce and distribute the poster. It is presented here in edited form.

THE JOURNAL

February 18

Woke up with a great idea, *The Last Yupper*. A poster with yuppies at da Vinci's *Last Supper* table. Dressed in yuppie garb, holding yuppie toys, eating yuppie foods. I know the term "Yupper" doesn't really mean anything, but it's close enough.

Sharon thought the idea was great, too. She immediately suggested we call Chuck and Lynn Shotwell, our good friends who run Charles Shotwell Photography. They're among the top commercial photographers in the city, and Chuck has done some posters. Sharon's reasoning: this would be a big undertaking and we know nothing about photogtaphy or posters. It would be fun to do it with friends, she said, but if it required going into business with strangers, it might not be worth it.

Before calling, we got out an art book with a picture of the da Vinci. It really is perfect. We would have our yuppies in the same poses as the apostles. There are terrific creative possibilities.

We talked to Lynn Shotwell early in the morning. She burst out laughing the minute we told her the idea and sounded like she would love to do it. She said she would talk to Chuck and call back. While waiting for the return call, I started playing around with some numbers. Surely, we could sell 50,000 of these things. Let's say we sold them at $20 apiece. That's $1 million!!!

Lynn called back and burst the bubble. Chuck thinks the concept is funny, but says it would cost a lot to produce the poster and that you can't make very much in the poster business. Several of his photographs have been made into posters by one of the top distributors in the country. About 1,000 posters are sold a year, and Chuck gets about $1 per poster.

I'm not that discouraged by those numbers. Chuck's posters are more artsy; ours would be a fad-type item. If it struck the right chord with people — are they on the same wavelength as we are? — it could sell thousands. Still, we do have to think about distribution. Would we want to handle that ourselves, to reap the biggest profit?

The discouraging thing about Chuck's response is that if he can't be persuaded to join the project, we'll either have to drop it or find someone else (whom we really wouldn't know) to be our partner. Chuck has agreed to meet this weekend to discuss the idea. In the meantime, we're all sworn to secrecy. As Sharon noted, if the phrase got out, it could turn up as a cartoon in the *New Yorker* before we can even produce a poster. The tough thing about keeping it secret is this: how can we tell if anyone else thinks it's a great idea? I'd hate to go to the expense and trouble of doing the poster only to find no one else liked the joke. Quite honestly, though, I don't think that will happen. I have to believe there are thousands and thousands of people out there who love this and want to buy it.

Would I buy it? I haven't bought a poster for years, but I think I would buy this, if not for our house, then for a gift. For $20? I don't know. But the price is something that can be worked out.

February 23

The Shotwells are coming for brunch tomorrow. Sharon and I have worked out our strategy. We have to convince Chuck that this will be a fun project that will give us all an opportunity to work together. We've always talked about doing that. Certainly we'll be able to sell enough posters to break even; whatever happens after that is gravy.

In my spare time this week, I've been playing with the picture, writing down the different kind of yuppie stereotypes we'd want in the poster and the different kinds of "props" they'd have. Sharon and I have also been trying to think which of our friends might be appropriate to appear in the poster. We know Dick Coughlin, our stockbroker, is a must.

I've also been thinking about financing. Lynn Shotwell said she would try to bring a budget indicating how much it would cost just to produce the poster. If we don't want to put up all the money ourselves, I'm certain we could raise the money from friends and family. Sharon isn't too enthusiastic about that. She says the only thing worse than losing our money would be to lose other people's money. I told her I had already lost other people's money before — on the wheelchair film — and that it *was* terrible. But as I kept apologizing over and over again to my investors, they kept telling me they went into the project knowing the risks, that no one held a gun to their heads, and that business had nothing to do with our friendships. I could go back to them for this. In fact I wouldn't mind, because I'm so confident about it.

February 24

I don't know if it was the bagels and lox or the sweet talk, but Chuck Shotwell is in! He's not convinced we'll make any money on the project, but he doesn't think we'll lose anything either. And he knows we'll have fun. He brought over some of the posters he's done. They are superb. If we had had to start from scratch and find a photographer, we would have probably ended up at his doorstep. He also brought over some of the contracts he has executed with the poster distributor. The small percentage Chuck receives reflects the fact that after he takes the photograph he turns the negative over to the distributor, who handles and pays for everything else — the costs of producing the poster from the image and then distributing the finished product. There is obviously a greater potential for profit if we produce and distribute the poster ourselves.

Chuck also brought the catalog of the company that distributes his posters and hundreds of others. The posters are very impressive. As Chuck pointed out, few, if any, are trendy like ours. He thinks the distributor might not want such a novelty as ours. In that event, we would probably have to distribute it ourselves.

The Shotwells apologized but said they wanted to make it clear up front that they are so busy with their regular business that they would have no time to market the poster. I wish I'd had that kind of honest communication with my partner in the courtroom videotape business. We never really established what each of us hoped to get out of the business and what each of us could contribute. I like marketing. I told Chuck and Lynn that that would be the least I could do after they produced a terrific poster.

Lynn had done a budget that indicated the costs if we produced the poster. The budget indicates where the expenses will be: getting a backdrop that matches the background in the da Vinci, getting props, film and other related photography expenses, paying a graphic artist to design the poster itself (I hadn't even thought of that!), and printing. We all agreed that there should be no money budgeted for their work or ours, whether we raise money from outsiders or finance it ourselves. We want to keep expenses down as much as possible if there are outsiders, and it wouldn't make too much sense to pay ourselves if we're the only investors. On this score, the Shotwells are in Sharon's camp. They don't relish the idea of soliciting friends or relatives.

We decided to use friends rather than professional models. As there are thirteen characters in the picture, models would be quite expensive. Besides, we know enough people who look like yuppies even if they shun the title.

We ended by planning another meeting for next Sunday. During the coming week we're all going to think of what yuppie look should go in the poster in what spot and whom we know that has that look. We're also going to think about particular props — yuppie toys like the Walkman and yuppie food and beverages like goat cheese and bottled water.

March 3

We met with the Shotwells again. We'd all done our homework. Lynn had a lengthy list of props for the poster — cellular phone, trivia game, kiwi fruit — and Sharon and I had ideas about what kind of yuppies should go where. We want the poster to be contemporary so we are adding women. As of now, we plan to have two working women, one of whom is pregnant, and a woman in an exercise outfit. We're thinking about putting this woman in a Jane Fonda–type top and having her sit in Judas's seat. After all, Jane seems to have betrayed, somewhat at least, her previously stated ideals in order to sell videos! In the rest of the spots, there will be, among others, a male jogger wearing a Walkman, a man holding a baby in a Snugli, a man videotaping the event, several people playing a trivia game, and a black businessman.

We are having a great deal of difficulty figuring out what to do with the central figure, who corresponds to Jesus Christ in the da Vinci masterpiece. We talked about putting him behind a *Wall Street Journal,* so we wouldn't have to show his face; we talked about superimposing the faces of celebrities as different as John Lennon and Gary Hart; we talked about having an old hippie there. Even though this is a humorous poster, we are taking it seriously. There should be a consistent theme if possible, although we don't want to get preachy.

We also talked about casting the poster. We went over our wedding pictures to find people with the right look. We agreed upon several, and will begin to call them this coming week. A March 31 shoot is our target.

March 6

Sharon solved the problem of the central figure. He will be a bearded figure in a three-piece suit. His hands will be outstretched just as Jesus' are in the da Vinci. But they won't be empty. In one hand, he will have the check; in the other hand he will have his American Express card. He will wear a pained expression on his face. "He's paying for the sins of the other yuppies' consumerism," explained

Sharon, who is a fiction writer and English Ph.D. student. "It's consistent with the da Vinci that way."

We know just the person for the center slot. Mike Dockterman, a nice Jewish boy from Rock Island, Illinois, is a physically imposing young lawyer with presence. He's the only person we can think of who can *fill* the space.

Still sworn to secrecy, we agreed that when we called our characters we would tell them only that we wanted them to pose in a poster and that they would not be asked to do anything obscene or embarrassing. We're counting on their sense of adventure. Since they're going to have to sign releases and will be paid $1 each, we certainly can't count on their greed! Dockterman is free on the date in question and gung ho. I told him he would be the star.

Lynn also had good news. She had found a top-notch set designer to paint the backdrop. It will have to be huge. A table for thirteen must sit in front of it. The designer can do the job relatively quickly and will charge us about $600. There was another alternative — we learned that one of the Shotwell's assistants had recently seen a photo of art directors in tuxedos posed at the Last Supper. Lynn called the photographer and found we could rent the backdrop used in that photo for about $575. We decided to have our own painted, so we could have it on hand to use again if necessary.

When I heard that there already was a contemporary version of the *Last Supper,* I was a bit worried. But it is not *The Last Yupper,* and it was just done as an in-house promotion at an advertising agency, not as a poster. Still, it makes me want to get going with this so we can beat to the punch anyone who might be thinking like we are. One of the entrepreneurs I interviewed for the book told me that at any one time dozens of people probably have the same idea. That's scary.

March 10

We met with the Shotwells for the third Sunday in a row. By now we know who we want in our cast. We've already called most of them, and everyone has accepted save Dick Coughlin, who we feel is essential to the poster. He *looks* like the stockbroker he is. We need him to hold the *Wall Street Journal* in one hand, while someone else passes him the cellular phone. Dick will be out of town on the thirty-first. We therefore decided to move the shoot up a week if he can do it then, assuming our central figure is still available.

We discussed marketing for the first time today. We think we can be very successful selling the poster mail-order. I have put together a list of magazines in which we might want to run ads. *New York* magazine, *Chicago* magazine, the *New York Times Sunday Magazine,* and the monthly magazines in several cities. I have also inquired about the rates at these magazines. Advertising is more expensive than I had figured. In most of these publications, it would cost $1,000 or more to take space for a small black-and-white photo ($2'' \times 3''$) of the poster. If we finance this ourselves, we may have to go without a photo and rely on the title and clever copy to generate the initial orders.

It appears that to produce and print between 1,000 and 5,000 posters will cost between $5,000 and $10,000. I've proposed that we budget another $10,000 for initial advertising. We don't have $20,000 to put up, but I'm confident we could set up a limited partnership. If we and the Shotwells put in $2,000 apiece, I think I could sell eight other $2,000 shares. We'd be general partners and take 50 percent of the profits in addition to having a smaller stake in the remaining 50 percent (by reason of our $2,000 investments). By putting up money ourselves, we'd convince the other investors of our belief in the project. We could also agree not to take any profit until the limited partners received their initial investments back. I bounced this idea off a lawyer friend who thought it sounded fine. But the Shotwells and Sharon are still reluctant to ask outsiders for money. I keep telling them we'd be doing our friends a favor to let them invest. We've decided to charge $20 a poster, and I'm still convinced we can sell tens of thousands. Even if we only sold a first run of 3,000, that would be $60,000. At that rate, assuming $20,000 in total expenses, each investor putting up $2,000 would make a 25 percent return on the investment. I have pages full of numbers.

March 19

The Shotwells called to say they have the backdrop and that it looks great. There may be a problem, however. There may not be enough space in their studio to give the photo the depth it needs. We have a backup. A friend with an office in an old loft has volunteered her space for our secret project.

The shoot is in just a few days, as both Coughlin and Dockterman were available for the twenty-fourth. We have called everyone in the cast to tell them what to wear. We're also having them bring a change of clothes so we can play with colors and styles. Needless to say, everyone is extremely curious. Dockterman is out of town, but due back soon.

March 21

Trouble. The Shotwells' studio won't do, and neither will our friend's loft. Lynn has found another studio for our Sunday shoot, but it will cost $300 to rent. That's $300 we weren't planning on spending.

Trouble. Two of our cast members are so busy at their jobs that they have decided to pull out. A third is questionable. And Dockterman, our star, is still out of town. His wife and secretary *think* he'll be back in time.

Everything was going so smoothly. It now occurs to me how tenuous this whole thing is. We've committed a fair amount of money already. The Shotwells have hired an assistant for the weekend; now the studio will cost money. If we have to scrub the shoot, it will be costly, and depressing, and worst of all, we may not be able to get the cast to assemble again.

Sharon will take the place of one person who can't make it and we've called a friend who says he thinks he can be on stand-by if we need him. I hope we don't.

March 23

I went and met Chuck and Lynn at the studio where we will shoot tomorrow. The backdrop was already up. It is terrific. It really looks like the background in the original. The table was set, too. Lynn has every touch perfect, from sushi to kiwi to chocolates to imported beers. We posed at the table for a few Polaroids so Chuck could get the camera set up for tomorrow. The photos looked great. It's amazing how the flat backdrop gives a feeling of depth.

I picked up some T-shirts I had ordered for the cast. In correspondence with the Shotwells, we have used the code name "Project Leonardo." That's what we had put on the T-shirts. Giving the cast T-shirts and a nice lunch after the shoot (we've budgeted about $250 for those two items) is the least we can do since they are working for a dollar.

Dockterman is back in town and will be there. We called our next door neighbor and she has agreed to fill the final spot. We're all very excited.

March 24

The shoot went great. Lynn had set a perfect table, and Chuck did a great job of getting thirteen nonprofessionals to look natural. He took several 8″ × 10″ Polaroids so we could play with the composition and poses. Then, when he was confident, he started shooting with regular film. Everyone in the cast thought the idea was terrific, leading me to believe we have a winner and that if we wanted we could probably tap a few of them to invest.

March 25

I woke up this morning thinking the whole project was a mistake, that I was crazy to think people were going to spend $20 for our poster. How had i been so foolish, so cocky?

March 26

Sharon and I went to the Shotwells' studio this morning to view the transparencies of the eighteen shots Chuck took two days ago. When I saw them, I felt confident once again. They were all so good. It took a long time for us to choose our favorite.

We have hired a graphic artist to design the poster. Her name is Susan Johnson, and she was one of the characters in the picture. She had so much fun at the shoot that I think she would do the work for free — she seemed to indicate that on Sunday. But she deserves to be paid. Besides, if she's paid she'll feel a greater responsibility to do it well and do it on time.

Time is important. Now that the cast and their families know about the secret project, word is bound to get out. The faster we can get the poster into production the better. Our marketing plan is to mail-order it ourselves and try to wholesale it to stores ourselves, at least initially. Then, we are confident, we'll be able to interest a national distributor or manufacturer's representative. We're confident that we can handle Chicago and that we may be able to interest friends in other major cities to distribute where they live.

April 25

Although the poster will not be ready for several more weeks, we decided to run a trial ad in the *Chicago Reader,* a free weekly tabloid with the kind of readers who should like our poster. The ad cost $228 and is about 5″ × 4″ black and white. The paper came out today. The photo reproduced fairly well on the newsprint, but you can't see any of the props clearly. Still, it's hard to miss the point. Sharon wrote the copy, which proclaims *The Last Yupper* as the "1985 State-of-the-Art Poster."

We set the price at $15, which includes taxes, postage, and handling. We have taken a post office box (I was surprised at how inexpensive it was). Checks are to be made to DaVinci Productions. We have decided to incorporate (to avoid personal liability), with Sharon and me and Chuck and Lynn as the shareholders. That will cost about $100 in state fees. The corporation will be capitalized with $1,000. Translation: each couple is buying $500 worth of stock to launch the effort, in addition to paying all the expenses. I did the incorporation papers myself, but even though I'm a lawyer, I checked with my accountant and a lawyer friend who specializes in corporate law before sending the form off. If we decide to set up a limited partnership with other investors, then DaVinci Productions will be the general partner.

We do not have a bank account yet, but that's okay. We are looking at the ad as a kind of trial balloon. The ad says to allow six weeks for delivery. If the response is terrible, we can always stop before going to the printer (where our major costs will come) and cut our losses. None of us expects that, but it does not hurt to have such a contingency plan. If we did decide to stop, we would refund the checks.

I think the ad is important for another reason, too. It is concrete evidence that we are in business. We are serious enough to have spent $228. Now let's move forward.

April 26

It will take about 20 poster sales for us to break even on the ad. I'm guessing that we can sell 50 to 100. Today, I decided to check the post office box, even though the ad just appeared last night. There was already one order. A good sign.

April 29

I went to the post office box expecting to find at least 20 poster orders. There were two. Two! What is wrong? Do people not respond to such ads? Do they have to actually see the poster? Is $15 too much? Is the concept just not as funny as we thought?

A friend said she couldn't tell much about the poster from the ad. That's troubling. How are we going to sell the poster by mail, if the ads we can afford can't attract orders?

There was one good sign. Channel Two, the local CBS affiliate, called. They had traced me by calling the post office (we don't have a corporate phone yet). The first question the fellow from the news asked was if there had been any religious controversy surrounding the poster. That is something that hadn't even occurred to us. I joked that there hadn't been but if it could get us on the news, I would try to stir things up. He told me to let him know when the poster was off the presses. We expect that to be the first week in June.

I have always thought the poster should make a good television and newspaper feature. Now, with the disappointing mail-order response, I think I'd better do something to make sure we get some coverage that will generate demand.

May 1

A few orders are trickling in, but it's so depressing that I've stopped going to the post office. I have been to the neighborhood bank where we have our personal checking account. I learned that it's expensive to open up a corporate checking account. There are charges for writing checks and making deposits unless you have a very large balance (so far we have only about $75!). Unwilling to pay these charges, I called the bank where our family has long done business and where I have a different corporate account. They will open an account that will have no such fees.

To build a little confidence in the venture and a little money in the bank, I have created a direct-mail offer to our out-of-town friends and some local ones as well. We're offering them the poster for $12. We will send out about 100 letters. That should start the ball rolling.

May 3

I think I've come up with a good plan to attract media attention. We'll have a Yupperware party to unveil the poster to the public and the press. We'll hold it on a racquetball court at a health club, the new yuppie temple. We'll invite all our friends and sell the posters at a special opening-night rate. As soon as we know when the posters will be ready, we'll set a date. We do have a printer. Susan Johnson, our artist, has been shopping around and found a highly regarded company that will do the work at a reasonable rate. We could get it done cheaper at a few other places, but we want the quality to be first-rate. We feel our audience, whoever that is, will demand that.

I showed the color transparency of the poster to a fellow I know who owns a yuppie-oriented bar and restaurant. I was hoping he might want to buy hundreds for a promotion. He didn't, but he loved the poster and told me he would like to take it to friends at a major retail chain. He asked me how we were going to package it, shrink-wrapped for example, and I said I had no idea. That hadn't even occurred to me. He also directed me to a friend of his who is a poster distributor. I'll call next week for an appointment. I showed the transparency to a few more people. They all loved it. Interestingly, about half said they thought yuppies would love it, and the other half said they thought anti-yuppies would love it. Maybe that's a problem. Maybe we fall between markets.

May 9

I met with the poster distributor in a large factory on Chicago's West Side. We sat in a back room surrounded by slick posters of Loni Anderson and souped-up cars. He liked the transparency and said we either had a poster which would retail for $2.50 or a *print* that would retail for around $8.00. He called a friend on the East Coast and told him he thought he might be able to sell 50,000 of them. My eyes lit up. Then he told me that the standard distribution contract would give us 10 percent of the wholesale price. A $2.50 poster may wholesale for 40¢. That would give us 4¢ a poster. He could sell 100,000 at that rate and we wouldn't break even.

I was noncommittal. He said he was going to be meeting in New York with some poster distributors and that he would let me know if they were interested and if we had a poster or a print. He was a nice guy and asked me what we were paying the printer. When I told him, he said we were paying too much. I called Susan Johnson and asked her to hold off with our printer until I heard the distributors' verdict. That will set production back a few days, but it seems worth it to see what the distributors think.

May 13

I went to the post office box for the first time in about a week. There were a few individual orders and an order from WFYR, a local radio station. The order was for one poster, but there was a letter from

Dick Rakovan, the station's general manager, asking about the possibility of buying more than one. I called him immediately, and within a few hours was in his office showing him the transparency. He liked it very much. He talked about buying a few hundred to give to clients and time-buyers. I told him we could sell that quantity for about $5 a poster.

May 14

I called Dick Rakovan and told him that if he ordered 1,000 posters I could give him a terrific deal.

May 15

Hurray! Rakovan and a sister station in Boston will split 1,000 posters. That will almost pay for a first printing of 3,000 posters. And if two stations want the poster, why shouldn't more want it? I called Susan Johnson and told her to move forward with our printing. Then I called a friend who is the general manager of a radio station in New York City. He may be interested. Then I called Channel Two to tell them we had already sold 1,100 posters (we've sold about 100 via the ad and our direct mailing, mostly the mailing). I told them we are unveiling the poster on June 7 and will soon be sending out a press release (we're doing that ourselves). Channel Two wants to do an exclusive on us on June 6. Fine. Finally, I called the telephone company. If we're going to get press coverage, we'd better have a phone so people can find us.

May 23

Our first press clipping. One of Sharon's students at Northwestern University works for the school newspaper and did a nice feature on us. We also received a call from *Chicago* magazine, the perfect forum. They responded to our press release and want to run a brief story and picture in the July issue. That should sell a lot of posters.

June 5

Ten proofs came off the presses today and the full order of 3,000 will arrive tomorrow, in time for our June 7 opening. 1,000 of those will go to the radio stations (the one in New York has turned us down for the time being) and 2,000 will go to our living room. That alone is incentive enough to sell them!

The poster, so big, so colorful, looks terrific. The Shotwells and Susan Johnson and the printer did a fantastic job. We had a scare with the printer a few weeks ago. There was some question whether the posters could be done in time. As we had already invited the press and about 150 friends to our opening, the posters had to be ready. When we politely suggested we might have to find another printer, the problem was solved.

I took one poster over to Artists Frame Service, a Chicago framing shop that also sells posters. The owner, Jay Goltz, liked the poster and said he would try to interest other poster shops in it. He was confident he could sell fifty to each of a few stores. He told me how pricing works in the poster business. If we price the poster at $20 retail as he suggests, our wholesale rate on orders of fifty or more will be $5 per poster. On smaller orders it will be $10. And if we continue to mail-order it ourselves, we will have to sell it for at least $20; it is not fair to undercut the retailers. So, it seems we'll have to sell a lot more than 50,000 posters to become millionaires!

June 6

Our second clipping. A local newspaper chain that had received our press release ran a page-wide picture of the poster and announced our Yupperware party.

Channel Two came and did the story and we were on the ten o'-clock news. It wasn't exactly what we expected. We thought there would be a soft feature on the yuppie craze. Instead, this was a "hard news" story about, as the anchorman said, "a poster creating quite a bit of controversy in Chicago."

How could a poster not even unveiled or in any stores create controversy? We had given the station an advance copy of the poster. It had taken the poster to the Catholic Archdiocese of Chicago and found a nun who thought the poster mixed religion with "a philosophy of self-aggrandizement." We were asked to defend ourselves. We told the reporter no harm was intended. We were contemporizing a painting, not a Bible illustration, that had been created 1,500 years after the event it portrayed. Sharon noted that since the central figure was dismayed at the check — sad to be paying for the sins of consumerism — the poster was actually consistent with Catholic theology.

We watched the news at home. The phone never stopped ringing. All of our friends, several of them Catholic (as are Sharon and several of the cast members), found the story a big to-do about nothing.

June 7

The phone started ringing before 9 A.M. Poster stores that had seen us on the news wanted the poster. The Associated Press wanted to take a picture of the unveiling. Jay Goltz told us two stores he had talked to wanted fifty posters each.

While waiting for the party to begin, I called another major store to try to sell some more posters. The manager said he might call back today, or he might call back next week to let me know. About an hour later, impatient to know if he had decided, I called and without identifying myself asked if the store was carrying the poster I had seen on the news last night. To my surprise, the answer was yes. A few minutes later, the manager called back and did indeed order some posters.

We sold about 120 posters and grossed about $1,000 at the opening. All of our friends seemed to enjoy the poster and the party. Some asked us to sign the poster. Several strangers showed up, having seen the announcement in yesterday's paper. A few people inquired about becoming distributors. We're not too far from break-even. We're all confident that we're over the hump.

Postscript

The roller coaster ride continued. The very next day we set up a table on a street near an art fair and tried to sell our poster to passers-by. We didn't sell very many. People enjoyed the poster. They stopped and spent a great deal of time going over the props and the characters. Most laughed, but didn't buy. We felt as though we were a museum and should have charged admission instead of trying to sell the poster. Admittedly, our location was not the best. Still, we began to wonder if we had produced a poster that would elicit smiles, but not checks.

Then, the next week, United Press International called. The wire service was doing a feature on yuppies and wanted to interview us and use a photo of the poster to accompany the story. The feature eventually ran in several newspapers, and we received calls and orders from people and stores from Winston-Salem to New Orleans.

About this time, we also approached a large chain of poster stores. The regional manager with whom I met looked me in the eye and said, "You are going to be a millionaire." He talked about ordering 1,000, but his home office told him to buy 50.

We have not become millionaires, but we have made a little money and had a lot of fun. The poster was eventually turned into a greeting card, too.

Wrapping posters and filling out United Parcel Service forms, I was reminded of Elaine and Arnold Cogan. Surveying 2,000 posters on our dining room table, I thought of Lynn Tatar. Trying to market the poster in my spare time as I wrote this book, I marveled at Duvall Hecht.

Finally, I thought of all the entrepreneurs who had told me that making money, while an undeniably pleasant by-product of their efforts, was neither their primary motivation nor goal. At some point early in the process, profit ceased being my motive as well. The process itself, making something out of nothing, is what drives you forward.

The words of Chaucer, written some 600 years ago, came to mind once again. "For he that naught n'assaieth, naught n'acheveth." Chaucer's knights live today. They are the men and women who dare to turn their great ideas into realities.

Resource Guide

REGIONAL OFFICES OF THE SMALL BUSINESS ADMINISTRATION

Region I
Boston Regional Office
60 Batterymarch, 10th floor
Boston, MA 02110

Region II
New York Regional Office
26 Federal Plaza, Room 29-118
New York, NY 10278

Region III
Philadelphia Regional Office
One Bala Cynwyd Plaza
Suite 640 West
231 St. Asaphs Rd.
Bala Cynwyd, PA 19004

Region IV
Atlanta Regional Office
1375 Peachtree St., N.E., 5th
   floor
Atlanta, GA 30367

Region V
Chicago Regional Office
230 S. Dearborn St., Room 510
Chicago, IL 60604

Region VI
Dallas Regional Office
8625 King George Dr.
Building C
Dallas, TX 75235-3391

Region VII

Kansas City Regional Office
911 Walnut St., 13th floor
Kansas City, MO 64106

Region VIII

Denver Regional Office
Executive Tower Bldg., 22nd
   floor
1405 Curtis St.
Denver, CO 80202-2395

Region IX

San Francisco Regional Office
450 Golden Gate Ave.
Box 36044
San Francisco, CA 94102

Region X

Seattle Regional Office
Fourth & Vine Bldg., Room 440
2615 Fourth Ave.
Seattle, WA 98121

UNIVERSITY EVALUATION CENTERS AND INVENTORS' ASSOCIATIONS

University Evaluation Centers

MIT Enterprise Forum
77 Massachusetts Ave.
Cambridge, MA 02139

Carnegie-Mellon University
Center for Entrepreneurial
   Development
4516 Henry St.
Pittsburgh, PA 15213

Massachusetts Institute of
   Technology
Innovation Center
Room 33-111
Cambridge, MA 02139

University of Utah
Utah Innovation Center
Office of Business
391 G So. Chiteta Way
Salt Lake City, UT 84112

California State University at
   Fresno
Bureau of Business Research
Fresno, CA 93740

Industrial Technology Research
   and Development Foundation
P.O. Box 1335
132 North Twelfth
Durant, OK 74701
(affiliated with Oklahoma State
   University)

Center for Private Enterprise
and Entrepreneurship
Hankamer School of Business
Suite 308
Baylor University
Waco, TX 76703

Center for New Business
Executives
Innovation Center
P.O. Box 12793
Research Triangle Park, NC
27709
(affiliated with University of
North Carolina)

Wisconsin Innovation Service
Center
402 McCutchan
University of Wisconsin
Whitewater, WI 53190

Center for Innovation and
Entrepreneurial Development
209 Classroom Bldg.
University of California
Santa Cruz, CA 95064

Center for Entrepreneurship
Wichita State University
Wichita, KS 67208

Inventors' Associations

American Society of Inventors
134 Narberth Ave.
Room 101
Narberth, PA 19072

California Inventors' Council
Box 2096
Sunnyvale, CA 94087

Central Florida Inventors' Club
2511 Edgewater Dr.
Orlando, FL 32804

Inventors' Assistance League
345 West Cypress
Glendale, CA 91204

Inventors of California/National
Innovation Workshop
P.O. Box 158
Rheem Valley, CA 94570

Inventors' Workshop
International
Box 251, Tarzana, CA 91356
and
32-22 92nd St.
Queens, NY 11369

Illinois Inventors' Council
53 W. Jackson
Chicago, IL 60604

Minnesota Inventors' Congress
Box 71
Redwood Falls, MN 56283

Mississippi Society of Inventors
Box 2244
Jackson, MS 39205

Oklahoma Inventors' Congress Technology Transfer Society
Box 53043 11720 W. Pico Blvd.
Oklahoma City, OK 73162 Los Angeles, CA 90064

Note: The services offered by the different University Evaluation Centers and Inventors' Associations vary. Some of these organizations are oriented toward high-technology innovations; some are not. Some may be helpful from the time an idea is formed to the time the product is on the market; some may be helpful for a shorter period. Remember, too, that several universities around the country have SBA Small Business Development Centers (SBDC). The SBA can refer the entrepreneur to the nearest SBDC. Finally, the free SBA pamphlet *Ideas into Dollars* is an excellent guide to services available to the innovator. It was a source for much of the information in this appendix.

Index